Richard L. Swanson

D1214616

ANTIQUE FURNITURE OF THE WALNUT PERIOD

PLATE I

Collection of Sir William Plender, G. B. E.

A lacquer cabinet of Oriental workmanship mounted on English carved wood and silvered stand, circa 1675.

ANTIQUE FURNITURE OF THE WALNUT PERIOD

BY

R. W. SYMONDS

AND

T. H. ORMSBEE

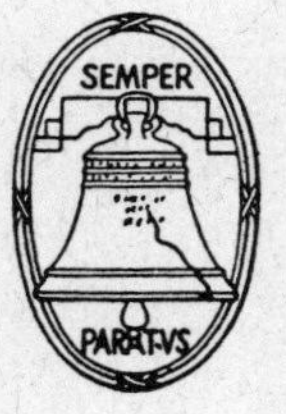

749.2
S

NEW YORK
ROBERT M. McBRIDE & COMPANY
1947

WITHDRAWN
Lakewood Memorial Library
Lakewood, N. Y.

ANTIQUE FURNITURE OF THE WALNUT PERIOD

Copyright 1947, by
Robert M. McBride & Company

Printed in the United States
of America

FIRST EDITION

PREFACE

When, as a complement to Mr. Symonds' chapters on antique English walnut and lacquer furniture, I undertook to write an account of the furniture colonial American craftsmen made in the same manner, it seemed a simple job of antiquarian research and reporting. Before the work was completed, however, it had proved most complex.

To begin with, there was a difference of some thirty years in timing. Next, there was the matter of woods. American craftsmen were not confined solely to walnut as were their English brethren, but had at their disposal a wide range of excellent woods suitable for cabinetry. Therefore, in addition to walnut, they executed much fine work in several other native hardwoods, notably maple, cherry, birch, and sometimes a combination of two or more of them in one piece.

Such being the case, in telling their story in Part II, the objective has been to present an account of furniture American cabinetmakers made that reflected the style of the English walnut period, noting especially what woods were used in making these pieces and what modifications of design and structure took place in the process.

Similarly, colonial America was not closely knit. It stretched in a thin fringe along the Atlantic seaboard from Maine to Charleston, South Carolina, with nothing resembling roads in the modern sense. Even the King's highways that connected the colonies were little better than bridle paths. Most travel was by coastal sailing vessels and these followed no fixed schedule of time or ports of call.

Consequently, interchange of information about new furniture designs, or anything else for that matter, was limited and colonial cabinetwork in general had marked regional characteristics. As a result, it is fairly easy today to distinguish pieces of New England provenance from those of New York, New Jersey or Pennsylvania, or the same in reverse. Also, because of the difficulty of travel by land or sea, most furniture was made by workmen living close by their customers. A good proportion was the work of village cabinetmakers and therefore was simple in line and detail as compared with more elaborate pieces from such centers as Boston, Newport, New York and Philadelphia.

All of this, I have endeavored to include as it is essential in any description of American furniture made between the emigrant century and the advent of the Chippendale period.

T.H.O.

CONTENTS

LIST OF ILLUSTRATIONS

LIST OF ILLUSTRATIONS

LIST OF ILLUSTRATIONS

LIST OF ILLUSTRATIONS

LIST OF ILLUSTRATIONS

LIST OF ILLUSTRATIONS

LIST OF ILLUSTRATIONS

ANTIQUE FURNITURE OF THE WALNUT PERIOD

ANTIQUE FURNITURE OF THE WALNUT PERIOD

CHAPTER I

WALNUT FURNITURE

1660–1745

THE high estimation in which old English walnut furniture is held at the present time is undoubtedly due to the appreciation of its artistic design and form, the natural beauty of the walnut wood with its fine figure and grain, and the beautiful mellow colour and patina which it has acquired by age. It is this variety of qualities, combined with the high standard of workmanship which prevailed throughout the walnut period, that entitles walnut furniture to be considered as the most artistic that England has produced.

Another reason which accounts for the popularity of old walnut furniture to-day, is the decorative value that it has in a modern room, in addition to its being as suitable for our requirements as it was for those of our ancestors. This appreciation has caused the monetary value of walnut pieces to increase considerably during the last few years, more so in fact than in the case of oak or mahogany furniture.

The steady rise in value of old English furniture during the last thirty or forty years and the present tendency towards a still further increase, taken in conjunction with the fact that the quantity of existing genuine furniture cannot be increased and is certain, as time goes on, to decrease, permits one to predict that fifty years hence old English furniture will be still more valuable than it is now. The value of old furniture will always depend on the demand for it, but it is not too much to assume that future generations will show an appreciation and regard for the furniture of our ancestors at least equal to that which animates the collector of to-day.

Lakewood Memorial Library
Lakewood, N. Y.

As an example of the lack of regard in which walnut furniture was held one hundred years ago, there exists a record in a sale catalogue, when the furniture and contents of Wanstead House, Essex, were sold by auction in the year 1822, of a set of ten walnut chairs with two settees only realizing the sum of £13 7s. In the same sale " A set of 8 solid mahogany carved frame scroll backed chairs, seats stuffed in beautiful yellow ground needlework, on lion's paw feet and balls," was sold for £2 12s. 6d. From the description the walnut suite of furniture would to-day be worth at least £700 and the mahogany chairs with their needlework covers would not be considered expensive at £100 a chair. The want of appreciation at that period is not, however, surprising, when one remembers that it was the dawn of an epoch which not only utterly forgot the artistic glories of the preceding century, but was completely lacking in any artistic inspiration of its own.

A notable fact in connection with walnut furniture is the quantity of it which is in existence. In nearly every small antique furniture shop throughout the country one is certain to find at least one, if not two or three, genuine pieces of walnut ; and in nearly every auction sale of antique furniture there are certain to be several examples.

At the beginning of the walnut period, in the reign of Charles II, the total population of England did not exceed five and a half millions, and the walnut period during which furniture was made of this wood came to a close about 1745, having lasted, therefore, only eighty-five years. When this is realized and consideration is given to the fact that a large percentage must have been destroyed by fire, or otherwise damaged and broken up (this fate has undoubtedly accounted for hundreds of pieces during the last one hundred and fifty years) and shiploads have been exported to the United States of America within recent years, the quantity that still remains in this country is truly remarkable.

Out of this comparatively large residue, however, it is, unfortunately, only a small portion that the discerning collector will wish to acquire, as a large amount of walnut furniture extant consists of parts of pieces, or pieces that have been very much restored, or have had their surfaces coated with a thick varnish, or that have been scraped and French polished. It is this last pernicious practice that accounts for the ruination of so much of the walnut furniture that is in existence to-day. French polishing destroys the mellow tone and colour of the walnut wood and the translucent effect which its surface has acquired through the action of time. These qualities, so important to the informed collector of walnut furniture, compose what is called " Patina."

Patina can only be acquired through the lapse of years, and is partly caused by the wood assuming a mellow tone through exposure to the air and the light, and partly due to the rubbing, dusting, and handling which the piece has received during its lifetime. To understand the alteration in the colour of walnut furniture, it must be realized that after a piece had been made, the surface was stained to give it an even tone of colour and to bring out the natural beauty of the figure of the wood, and then finished with a thin coat of transparent varnish or polish. Long exposure to the light causes the varnish to assume a tone which gives a light mellow golden colour to the wood. The light also draws out the colour of the stain which was applied to the piece when made, and turns the outer skin of the wood to a light tone. In cases where a piece has stood in the sunlight for a number of years, the colour fades to an almost grey hue; the sun's action, besides bleaching the skin of the wood, having also perished the varnish.

As an example of an effect of bleaching on a piece of walnut, it will be seen that in Plate XIV of a walnut table, the top part of the left-hand inner leg is much darker than the right-hand leg: this has been caused through the piece standing for a number of years with the top open beside a window where the right-hand leg has caught the sun, and the other leg being in the shadow, is in consequence unfaded and of a dark tone.

That it is the varnish, or polish, that gives the light golden colour to pieces of walnut is amply proved by the fact that in some cases where it has worn off, the wood thus exposed is darker in tone, as compared with the other parts.*

This alteration in colour through exposure to the atmosphere and light is also especially noticeable if one of the mounts of an untouched piece, such as a handle, is removed. If the handle is original, the wood behind the back-plate, having been covered up since the piece was first made, will be found to be of an entirely different tone and colour from the exposed surface of the piece. The colour of walnut pieces in their untouched state varies considerably from the golden brown colour, caused through the mellowing of the varnish, or polish, to the almost grey tone of the piece which has become faded through the action of the sun's rays upon it. There is no doubt that this alteration of the original colour of the wood gives a beauty to the piece which it lacked when first made.

When the original surface is removed from a piece by a solvent—which is a necessary process before the piece can be French polished—the very attractive golden colour and the light tone of the wood are lost and no subsequent staining and polishing will succeed in recalling them. The wood becomes darker in tone and its surface raw, with the grain open.

* For an example of this see Plate XXIV of a walnut bureau bookcase where the polish has worn off at the bottoms of the doors through constant handling.

When a piece is French polished this open grain is filled up sometimes with plaster of Paris and sometimes with pumice-stone powder, until a perfectly smooth surface has been obtained. This surface then receives three or four coats of polish and is left with a smooth glass-like finish ; the figure of the wood becomes thereby obscured by the filling up of the grain and the heavy coatings of coloured polish, giving the piece a dark muddy appearance very far removed from the untouched example with its original golden colour. The French polish sinks into the surface of the wood and cannot be removed except by very drastic methods, whereas the old varnish, or polish, remains on the surface of the piece and can be scratched off.

The lighter, or bleached, pieces of walnut are now the most highly prized owing to their greater decorative value, which is especially enhanced by the figure and grain of the wood being more distinct than in the darker examples.

In addition to the change in the colour of the wood, the rubbing, dusting and handling that the surface of a piece has received since it was made, constitute a factor in the creation of its patina. This rubbing and dusting give to the surface of the wood a high gloss, very different from the artificial shine that is the result of French polish ; this gloss is the polishing of the varnish which, however, is so thinly applied that it is barely perceptible.

Another feature which belongs to pieces possessing patina and adds to their decorative value is the richness of tone given to the carving by the formation of a dark deposit, caused by the accumulation of dust and dirt, combined with the beeswax or oil which has been applied to the piece from time to time for the purpose of domestic cleaning.

For example, dust and dirt settling on the carved back of a Charles II chair, adhere to the beeswax which, on the less exposed surfaces of the carving, will not have been entirely removed by dusting. In course of time this beeswax gradually becomes hard and, darkened in tone by dust, acts as a foil to the raised parts which are light in tone in comparison, for, owing to their relief, they will have been rubbed clean by the duster. The accidental effect of light and shade thus formed is a very attractive feature in carved walnut pieces, and is also noticeable in a lesser degree on the mouldings of plain pieces, such as a bureau-bookcase.

The importance to the collector of only buying pieces with good patina cannot be exaggerated, and if he confines his purchase to examples which have this desirable attribute not only will he be secure in the knowledge that his furniture possesses the additional beauty that patina confers, but that it is unquestionably genuine.

Naturally, if he studies design only, his choice of a piece will not be affected if it is French polished ; or, if fine workmanship be his standard of excellence, the absence of good surface condition will not weigh with him. But colour has an artistic value, as well as form and finish, and when a piece has had the mellow tone of age altered to a dark muddy colour, the change must be detrimental to its artistic value ; that it is detrimental to its commercial value is amply proved by the fact that the present-day value of walnut pieces is largely influenced by the excellence, or otherwise, of their patina.

Although by confining himself to buying pieces in their original state the collector considerably reduces his range of purchase, yet he will have the satisfaction of knowing that this self-imposed limitation is supported by sound artistic and commercial principles.

The high appreciation of patina is not due to faddism. It is true that the question of rarity arises in connection with it, because it is the quality most rarely found in walnut furniture, but, far transcending the importance of " rarity," recognition must be given to the inherent power it possesses of investing the whole of a piece of furniture with an indefinable beauty peculiar to itself and inimitable. Its appreciation, therefore, is not a matter of preciosity but of good taste, insight and fidelity to what is artistically true.

The walnut furniture extant shows a large quantity of certain types of articles and a great scarcity of others. The scarcity of some articles is due, undoubtedly, to their having been destroyed through their fragile construction being unable to withstand the vicissitudes of time; such, for example, are the stands for cabinets and chests. There are many chests and cabinets extant, but very few stands that supported them, as their delicate legs have been broken in the course of time and it is only the cabinet or chest that has survived. The large quantity of chairs that exist from the period of Charles II is especially noticeable, as also is the number of bureaux and bureau-bookcases from the latter half of the walnut period. Other examples that exist in large numbers to-day are such pieces as chests-with-drawers, tallboys and small pedestal dressing-tables and the small dressing-table on legs, all of which can be classified as bedroom furniture.

Another type of article which has come down to us in large numbers is the long-case walnut clock. On the other hand, the scarcity of walnut tables, bookcases and china cabinets throughout the whole period is very noticeable.

The varying scarcity and abundance of different pieces of walnut furniture is to some extent compensated for by the fact that where there is a paucity of one particular type of piece in walnut, there is a corresponding abundance of the similar piece in either oak or mahogany ; and conversely

PLATE II

(Left) A walnut arm-chair, circa 1660. (The turned-back stretcher is not original.) *Collection of Cecil Millar*

(Right) A walnut arm-chair, circa 1665. *Collection of Sir John Prestige*

where there is an abundance in walnut there is a scarcity in oak or mahogany. As an example of this, there is a comparatively large number of oak gate-legged tables of the late seventeenth century, and a negligible quantity in walnut; again, later in the period, there is a large quantity of mahogany side-tables and oval-top dining-tables, but a contemporary example in walnut is of extreme rarity. The great quantity of walnut bedroom furniture, such as has already been specified, may be contrasted with the absence of contemporary mahogany examples; and similarly it is also very noticeable as regards long-case clocks, bureaux and bureau-bookcases.

From this it would appear that houses were furnished with oak and walnut furniture from 1660—the beginning of the walnut period—up to the introduction of mahogany furniture about 1720, and from 1720–1745 with walnut and mahogany furniture. This would, of course, only refer to houses of the well-to-do, as the poorer classes throughout the walnut period used furniture made of oak, or fruit-wood, which is proved by the number of contemporary examples that have survived in these woods of a similar design to those in walnut.

It is difficult to offer an explanation for the reason that the cabinet-makers of the walnut period made certain articles only in oak and mahogany and not in walnut. Why such furniture as chests-with-drawers, tallboys, bureaux, bureau-bookcases, dressing-tables, and long-case clocks was made in walnut and not in mahogany is perhaps due to the fact that, when mahogany was first introduced, the cabinet-makers only used a variety which, although a splendid medium for carving, had but little figure or grain. They therefore employed this mahogany, which lacked the natural decorative feature possessed by walnut, for those pieces they intended to decorate with carving; and continued to use walnut for the plain pieces which would have been too monotonous in appearance if made in the unfigured mahogany. This is amply borne out by those plain pieces of this period that are met with to-day made in mahogany; being uninteresting and plain-looking, they can in no way compare in decorative value with the walnut examples. The cabinet-makers continued to make these plain pieces in walnut until they began to use Cuban mahogany, which had a fine figure and grain, and so combined the qualities of the two woods. A fact that helps to prove the truth of this theory is that furniture began to be made in fine-figured mahogany about 1745, after which date walnut practically ceased to be used for furniture making.

The abundance and scarcity of different pieces of walnut furniture naturally influences their monetary value to-day, the prevalence of some articles and the rarity of others being reflected in their respective costs; the value of a bureau, which is a comparatively common piece,

PLATE III

(Left) A walnut chair of unusual and elaborate design, probably of Dutch workmanship, circa 1685. *Collection of J. Thursby Pelham*

(Center) A tall walnut child's chair, circa 1667. *Collection of Sir John Prestige*

(Right) A walnut chair, circa 1675. *Collection of M. Harris*

being considerably less than that of a walnut table, which is a far rarer article.

As a general rule it will be noticed that the cabinet-makers of the walnut period did not vary, to any great extent, the shape and form of their furniture; when, therefore, a piece is discovered, which, because of some elaboration or unusual feature, differs from the pattern usually found, its value will be correspondingly high. In addition to following a similarity in design, the cabinet-makers more or less standardized their measurements, which is the reason why such pieces as bureaux, bureau-bookcases and chest-with-drawers are generally found to-day about 3 feet to 3 feet 6 inches in width. They also, however, made these pieces measuring from about 2 feet to 2 feet 6 inches in width, and these narrower examples are more sought after, partly because of their rarity, but also on account of the greater convenience they afford for modern requirements in small rooms.

Judging from examples that have survived, certain pieces appear to have been made only in small sizes. Examples of these are the small pedestal dressing-table, the dressing-table on legs and the rare small writing bureau on stand. It is difficult to say why the cabinet-makers did not make large examples of these pieces, especially of the dressing-table, which it is reasonable to suppose would have been more useful in the larger size.

Another feature which has an important influence upon the value of walnut furniture, in addition to patina, design and size, is the quality of a piece. This varies considerably, showing that just as there are pieces to-day in modern furniture varying to suit the purse of the purchaser, so there were in the walnut age. The details of this variation in quality will be more fully dealt with in the next chapter.

This question of gauging the quality of a piece is an important one to the collector, and an examination in this respect should always be made with a view to arriving at a correct estimate of its value. The question of "original" quality is quite independent of "patina," as, naturally, the two have no connection with each other, the one being given to a piece when made, the other acquired by it through age. To find both in a piece is very desirable, but, unfortunately, rare, and generally it is the latter that is lacking. Of the two the absence of patina is the more to be deplored, inferior quality being less detrimental to the appearance of a piece than the destruction of its patina.

Another point in connection with walnut furniture that is important to the collector is whether a piece is English or foreign. Walnut furniture was not made in England alone, as in Holland, France, Spain, and Italy, furniture was being made from this wood contemporaneously with the walnut period in England. The English were the last to adopt the use of walnut wood for their furniture, and, as will be seen, its introduction into this country was due to the English arts and crafts in the time of Charles II being strongly influenced by foreign tastes. The fact, therefore, that English walnut furniture was copied and adapted, both as regards its design and the manner in which it was made, from the furniture of foreign countries, gives it a similarity in appearance to foreign examples. The walnut furniture of English origin has a far higher value in England to-day than the majority of the contemporary foreign pieces, and this difference in some cases is so marked that it makes the question of the provenience of a piece one that requires serious consideration on the part of the collector, as he is likely to meet with a large quantity of foreign walnut furniture in this country which has been imported within recent years to meet the demand for English walnut. The collector, therefore, who intends to rely on his own judgment when he purchases a piece should make himself acquainted with the difference in design and execution between English furniture and the contemporary furniture of foreign origin.

As will be shown in the succeeding chapters, there is a great similarity between the English and Dutch examples belonging to the first half of the walnut period. In the last half the similarity is not so marked, as designers and makers of English furniture gradually freed themselves from foreign influence and began to evolve an individual style of their own. The difference in value between the later examples of Dutch and English furniture is greater than it is between the earlier.

Compared with the Dutch, the contemporary Spanish and Italian furniture does not bear so close a resemblance to the English, and, therefore, is less dangerous to the collector. The same remark applies, also, to the contemporary French walnut furniture, with the exception of some chairs and stools which bear a strong resemblance to the English examples of the period of William and Mary. Such French pieces, however, are but seldom met with in this country, and are in most cases as valuable as the English examples.

In the succeeding chapters reference will be made to the way the furniture designers and cabinet-makers in England followed and adapted the designs of the Dutch furniture, and also, though in a lesser degree, those of the French. The varying differences in construction and workmanship between the English and Dutch cabinet work is also mentioned. If Dutch and English examples are studied and examined on the lines indicated, the collector will soon acquire a knowledge of, and a familiarity with, the details in design and construction which are characteristic of the furniture of each country, so that recognition of a foreign example will not be difficult.

CHAPTER II

QUALITY AND WORKMANSHIP

THE construction and workmanship of walnut furniture from the beginning of the walnut period to the reign of Queen Anne was strongly influenced by the Dutch. This was due to the commercial intercourse between Holland and England, and the revival of the arts in this country after the Restoration, which stimulated the importation of Dutch furniture and the migration of a number of Dutch craftsmen to these shores. This influx of Dutch ideas and craftsmen considerably increased when William III became king, in fact, during his reign the palaces at Hampton Court and Kensington, and the houses of the nobility, were furnished and decorated in an Anglo-Dutch style.

At this period the craft of furniture making in England was undoubtedly, to a large extent, in the hands of Dutchmen, who were highly gifted as designers and cabinet-makers. One of the few surviving records of a cabinet-maker in the late seventeenth century mentions Gerreit Johnson, a Dutchman, who must have been one of the leading cabinet-makers in England, as he supplied several china cabinets to Queen Mary for her china closet at Hampton Court. The celebrated Grinling Gibbon, whose naturalistic wood-carving was so beautiful a feature of the oak panelled rooms of this period, was also of Dutch origin.

It is a notable fact, however, that English walnut furniture still retained an insular character, even though made by Dutch craftsmen in the Dutch manner, and in a style derived from foreign influences and made, in some cases, out of imported material. These Dutch immigrants, although they employed their own methods of construction and workmanship, invariably adapted the design of the furniture they produced to suit the taste and needs of the English market.

By the reign of Queen Anne the workmanship had become more refined and not so Dutch in character as in the first half of the walnut age. This improvement in the quality of workmanship continued until the end of the period, in proportion as the Dutch influence gradually declined. An example of this is seen in the manner of dovetailing in drawers of furniture of about 1680, which is so like that of the contemporary Dutch furniture that it would be impossible to determine the provenience of a piece from this feature alone. By 1715 the English form of dovetailing had not only altered in construction, but had become much finer than the contemporary Dutch, which still retained its original roughness of finish. The same peculiarity is also noticeable between the quality of early Dutch and English marquetry and the late marquetry of the two countries.

The introduction of Dutch methods of construction and Dutch workmanship in making English furniture is, at this period, distinctly marked by the use of "veneer," as previously all furniture in England had been made out of the solid wood. In the making of veneered furniture a carcase was first constructed of deal or oak and a layer of walnut (cut to about $\frac{1}{16}$ to $\frac{1}{8}$ of an inch in thickness) was then glued on to the surface. By this means the decorative value of the natural beauty of the figure of the wood was best obtained, the veneer being carefully arranged so that its figure formed a symmetrical pattern. To do this four pieces of veneer were cut in successive layers from the same piece of wood, so that each piece would have identically the same markings. The four were then laid together so that the markings joined and formed a symmetrical pattern. To cover a table-top, for instance, each of the four pieces would form a quarter of the whole top and, the markings being identical in each, a symmetrical pattern would thus be obtained. The cutting and laying of the veneer in this manner is termed "quartering."

The way in which the "veneer" was cut from the tree also gave a variation to the figure; for instance, if it were cut lengthways from the trunk it would show the grain running along the surface, whereas if the veneer were cut across the root of the tree, the figure would be far more finely marked and have a mottled appearance. Walnut cut in this latter manner is called "burr walnut." Another method of obtaining a variation of the figure, which was much in vogue during the first half of the walnut period, was by cutting the veneer transversely at an oblique angle from the smaller branches of the tree, which produced an oval figure, and from its resemblance to the shell of an oyster is termed "oyster-shell veneer." Each piece of veneer was skilfully cut to fit the adjoining pieces before they were glued to the carcase, and they were so arranged that the sections of the wood formed a pattern. A very favourite method of still further enhancing the appearance of this veneer was to inlay into its surface, after it had been glued on to the carcase, lines of holly or boxwood in a geometrical pattern. Cabinets, clock-cases, chests-with-drawers and the tops of tables will all be found decorated with this oyster-shell parquetry, and it was specially suitable for the flat stretchers of tables and stands owing to the small marking of the figure.

Examples with oyster-shell parquetry are naturally of a higher value than those decorated with the straight-cut veneer from the trunk. Laburnum was the wood most often selected for this particular treatment, having the best figure for the purpose ; walnut was not so suitable, the markings in the smaller branches not being sufficiently pronounced. Olive wood parquetry was sometimes used, and is generally met with on cabinet doors and on clock-cases ; while two other woods occasionally employed in this manner were coromandel and king wood. Lignum-vitæ was also made use of, but not often, owing to its dark colour.

Besides the careful arrangement of the figure, the surfaces of a piece, such as the top of a table or the door of a cabinet, were bordered by an edging of cross-banded veneer. This border, or edging, has the grain of the wood running across the width and not along the length. Inside this border, and dividing it from the central panel of veneer, a small band of herring-bone or feather inlay made of narrow strips of veneer cut on a slant is invariably found. These strips were laid side by side, so that the grain met in the middle at a right angle. This herring-bone or feather inlay was a much favoured type of decoration for walnut pieces, in fact it may be said that but few pieces of veneered walnut are ever found without it. It was invariably used on drawer fronts, sometimes in conjunction with, but more often without, the cross-banded edging described above. On the earlier pieces this inlay was wider than on the later.

After the carcase of the piece had been veneered the necessary mouldings were then applied. The mouldings were formed by glueing a narrow strip of cross-cut walnut on to a foundation of deal, the surface of the walnut being then worked to the required section. All these mouldings were cross-cut, that is to say, they had the grain running across the width and not along the length.

Sometimes the furniture of the walnut period, especially chairs, stools, settees, and mirror frames, had the mouldings and carving enriched with gilding. (For an example of a piece with the carved enrichment gilded see Plate XXV.) This was more often the case in the reign of Queen Anne and subsequently, but even then its use was reserved for the more expensive pieces, and but few genuine examples exist.

Occasionally the backs and legs of chairs and settees were decorated with an ornamental panel of gilt gesso. This feature was carved out of a thin coating of plaster in very low relief and then gilt, but very few examples of walnut furniture enriched in this manner are known,

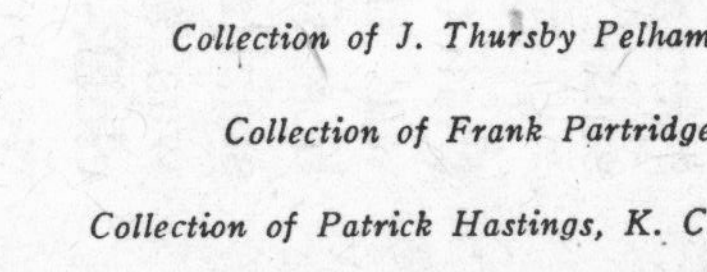

PLATE IV

(Left) A walnut chair, probably Dutch, circa 1695. *Collection of J. Thursby Pelham*

(Center) A beech arm-chair, painted black, circa 1685. *Collection of Frank Partridge*

(Right) A walnut chair with finely carved splats in back and serpentine stretcher, circa 1685. *Collection of Patrick Hastings, K. C.*

although the combination is not so scarce where walnut mirrors are concerned.

The gilding of this period was of the finest quality, and when new must have been bright and glaring. Time, however, has deprived it of some of its brilliance, and to-day, when found in conjunction with the walnut, both mellowed and patinated, the effect is the very reverse of garish, the subdued tone of the gilding being in perfect harmony with the walnut wood, and adding considerably to the beauty and value of the piece.

The way the present-day value of walnut furniture is affected by its quality has already been commented upon, and pieces can be divided into three classes according to the degree of quality that they possess. The first consists of costly pieces of superlative merit and of elaborate design made for the nobility, in which the finest workmanship and material have been employed throughout. In the second, representing the more ordinary type of furniture made for the well-to-do, the workmanship is of a high standard, but more restraint is shown in design and ornamentation. The third comprises pieces of poor and coarse workmanship made in an altogether cheaper manner from inferior materials and at much less cost.

The quality of a walnut piece is determined to a large extent by the marking and figure of the veneer. In a piece of high quality burr walnut or another type of finely figured walnut was used on the drawer fronts or door panels, a less figured veneer being employed for the sides, which were not so conspicuous or important as the front of the piece. In an example of inferior quality the front was treated with plain veneer cut from the trunk of the tree, which cost considerably less than the finely marked variety, and the sides in some cases were formed by the deal carcase stained to resemble walnut. In such a piece attention was not paid to the arrangement of the figure to obtain a symmetrical design, and the decorative value of the piece suffered accordingly.

Drawer linings of deal instead of oak are another feature which denotes a piece of poor quality. Sometimes the front of the drawer is made of deal with the sides, back and bottom of oak ; pieces with drawers made in this manner are not of such good quality as those which have their drawers lined entirely in oak. A further mark of good quality is when the sides of the drawers have their top edges carefully rounded off ; on an inferior piece they are either left square or with the sharp edges roughly removed.

In appraising the quality of a piece the amount of oak used in the construction of the carcase should always be noted. Oak was a better foundation for veneer than a soft wood such as deal, but it was more expensive, and therefore was sparingly employed, if at all, on cheaper grade pieces. As an example of this, the interiors of good quality bookcases and cabinets where the carcase can be seen will be made of oak, but where the carcase is not visible, as in the case of the bottom part of a bureau-bookcase, which is hidden by the drawers, it will generally be found made of deal. In a piece of inferior quality the exposed parts of the carcase are made of deal as well as the unseen parts.

The drawers of walnut furniture are nearly always found constructed so that the grain of the wood of the drawer bottoms runs from front to back; when the grain runs from side to side it shows that the piece must have been made about the middle of the eighteenth century or later, when drawers were first constructed in this manner. In the early walnut furniture of the time of Charles II the drawer bottoms were nailed to the bottom edges of the drawer sides, and the drawers had no runners,* but from the time of William and Mary onwards, the bottoms were let into rabbets cut in the bottom edges of the sides, and then strips of wood were glued on to the bottom drawer to act as runners, see Diagram 1. Many walnut pieces of this later time will also be found with the drawer bottoms and runners fixed to the bottom edges of the sides without the rabbets, but this method of construction denotes inferior workmanship, as it was both quicker and easier to fix the bottom in this manner than to cut the rabbets in the sides.

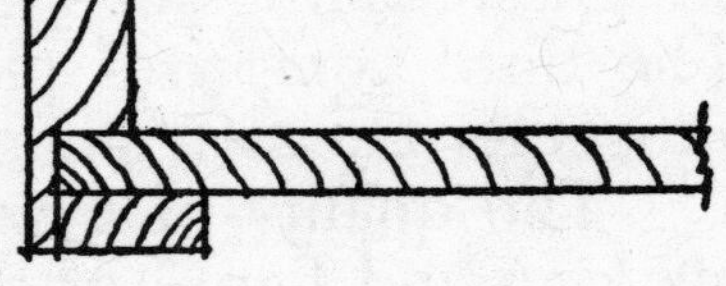

DIAGRAM 1.
Drawer bottom let into rabbet in drawer side.

The drawers of the furniture of the period of Charles II had the dovetails carried through to the face of the drawer front, and the dovetailing was coarse, there being only about three tails in the depth of the drawer (see Diagram 2)†; but in the drawers from the reign of William and Mary onwards the dovetails were not carried through in this manner, being stopped about $\frac{1}{4}$ inch from the face (see Diagram 3). Dovetailing of the latter type became finer as the eighteenth century advanced, the tails being increased in number and made narrower. The date of a piece can be roughly gauged by the dovetailing of the drawers. In English walnut pieces

* The construction of the drawers without runners is typical of oak furniture from Elizabeth to Cromwell, in which the drawer was carried on bearers or runners, fixed to the carcase, which slid in grooves cut in the drawer sides. The early type of drawer with this form of runner is sometimes found on walnut pieces of country make, but it is more typical of oak than walnut furniture, as this method was discarded in the best furniture from the time of Charles II, and thereafter was only followed by country cabinet-makers.

† Many pieces dating from the early part of the eighteenth century will be found with the drawers dovetailed in this earlier manner, such pieces being the work of country cabinet-makers. This earlier dovetailing will also be found on Dutch pieces, as it was a form of dovetail favoured by the Dutch long after it had been discarded by the English.

the drawers were always dovetailed and never nailed ; a piece with the drawers nailed together is indicated as a Dutch example.

The variation in the design of the mouldings or beads on or around the drawer fronts is a rough indication of the date of the construction of those walnut pieces that were fitted with drawers. The accompanying

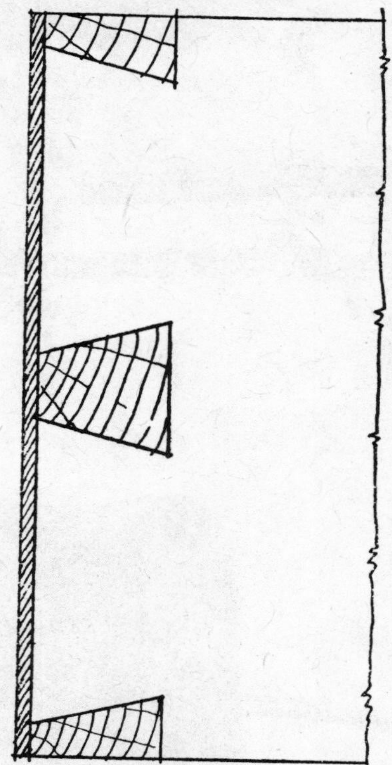

DIAGRAM 2.
Early form of dovetailing found in Charles II and James II walnut furniture.

DIAGRAM 3.
Later form of dovetailing found on English walnut furniture dating from the reign of William & Mary onwards

Diagrams, 4, 5, 6, 7, show the different mouldings and their dates. These dates, however, are only very approximate, especially as regards oak or fruit-wood furniture of country make, as the smaller country cabinet-makers in many cases continued to use methods and styles after their contemporaries in the larger towns had adopted fresh ideas.

Besides this veneered furniture, the making of which started in the

PLATE V

Collection of Percival D. Griffiths

(Top, left) A French walnut child's chair with upholstered seat and cane panel in back, circa 1685. (This foreign chair shows how closely the English chairs at this period were copied from the foreign models.)

(Top, right) A walnut nursing chair, circa 1670.

(Bottom, left) A walnut child's arm-chair, circa 1685.

(Bottom, right) A child's walnut arm-chair with upholstered back and seat, circa 1730.

first decade of the reign of Charles II, articles such as chairs, stools, and couches were made in solid walnut. These articles were decorated with carving and turning, and their production commenced just before the Restoration and continued up to the beginning of Queen Anne's reign. After this date the backs of chairs, instead of being carved, were

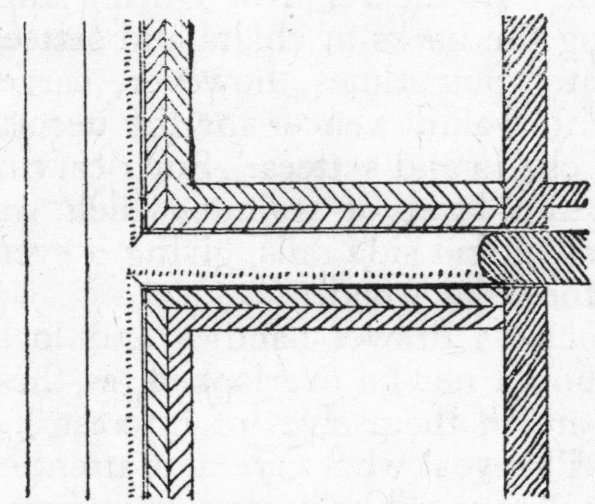

DIAGRAM 4.
Half round beading on carcase round drawer front.
Circa 1660 to 1705.

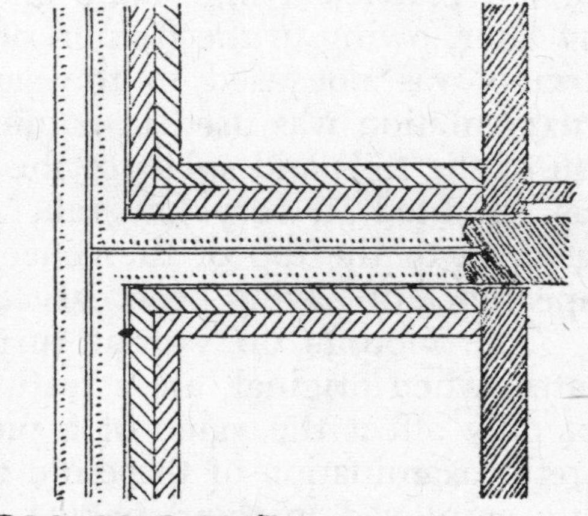

DIAGRAM 5.
Double halfround beading on carcase round drawer front.
Circa 1700 to 1715.

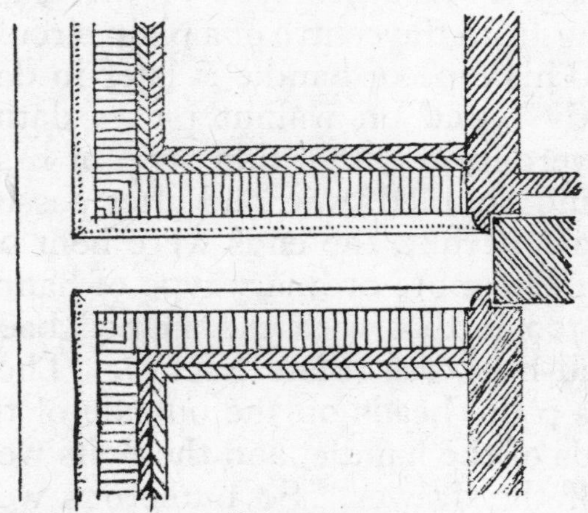

DIAGRAM 6.
Overlapping drawerfront with moulded edge.
Circa 1715 to 1735.

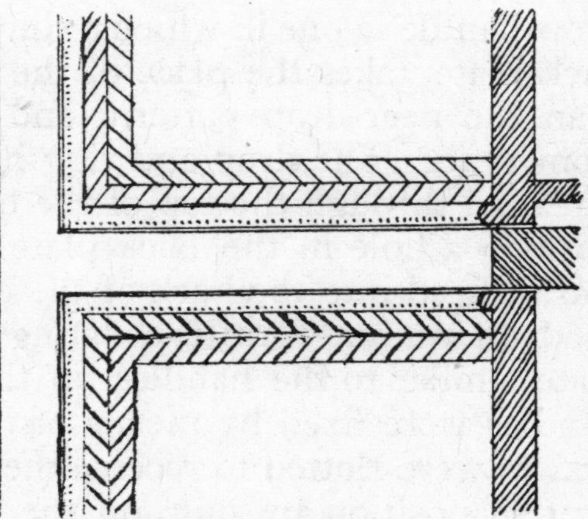

DIAGRAM 7.
Edge of drawer front surrounded by cock bead.
Circa 1730 to 1800.

veneered, together with the seat rails, the legs and arms only being in the solid.

There are degrees of quality in carving, as there are degrees of quality in veneered work. The quality of the carving was progressive in fineness of execution from the reign of Charles II to that of William III, in whose reign it reached a high state of perfection. In the reign of Queen Anne and later, owing to the fashion of veneering the backs of chairs and settees, carving was not used to the same extent. Sometimes, however, carved ornamentation was used in conjunction with walnut veneer for the decoration of the rails and splats of the backs of chairs and settees. Such carving was executed in very low relief from a thin layer of walnut which was glued on to the top of the veneer of the splat and side rails, giving it every appearance of having been carved out of the solid wood.

The mounts on walnut furniture, such as drawer-handles and lock-plates, when original, are a feature that should not be overlooked, as these not only affect the value of a piece, but are in themselves of interest. A careful examination of these old mounts will reveal what care and attention were employed in their making. They will invariably be found in brass, lacquered so that they should not become dull through exposure to the atmosphere or require constant cleaning. The earliest type of drawer-handle in the walnut period was the single drop ; it was made in a number of different designs, but genuine examples, when found, are usually of what is known as the "Pear-drop" pattern. Examples of drop handles are shown on Plates VIII (*c*), XXXIV (*a*) and XXXVI (*a*). Another type of the single drop-handle is one in which a ring, hanging from the centre of a plain circular back-plate, takes the place of the drop. This type of handle is later in date than the pear-drop pattern, and is mostly found on walnut pieces dating from 1720. The drop and ring handles were fixed with a thin strip of brass threaded through the top of the handle, and doubled over, and after passing through a hole in the back-plate and drawer front, the ends were bent out and pressed into the back of the drawer. The more ordinary type of handle used on walnut furniture dating from 1700 is that with the shaped back-plate similar to the handles on the bureau-bookcase (Plate XXIV). These handles were fixed by means of two bolts ; the heads on the outside of the drawer were slotted to receive the two ends of the handle, and the bolts were kept in position by nuts on the inside of the drawer. So numerous were the designs for the back-plates to this type of handle that it is seldom to-day that two pieces which have their original mounts are found with the back-plates of the same design.

The lock-plate or escutcheon was always made *en suite* with the back-plate, and fixed to the drawer front by small brass pins. Sometimes these handles and lock-plates are decorated with an engraved design, and when they are of good quality their presence on a piece adds to its interest. The early examples of this type of handle with a back-plate are small, but towards the end of the walnut period they became larger. The larger ones sometimes had the back-plates pierced with a fret design or with the centre cut away in order to lighten their appearance (Plate XXV). These mounts varied in quality according to their original cost ; the cheaper ones lacked the finish of the better examples, the engraving, if any, being crude, and the plates thin with rough edges. On pieces of furniture of very fine quality the mounts were water gilt instead of being lacquered.

The quality of the original locks also varies considerably. The better examples are of brass, well made and nicely finished ; whereas the cheaper locks were made of iron, of coarse workmanship and rough in appearance.

A difference that exists between the English and Dutch locks, and which is of assistance in determining whether a piece is Dutch or English, is that the Dutch lock is deeper from top to bottom, and the keyhole is, consequently, further removed from the top of the drawer.

From the above brief remarks it will be seen that the handle and lock-plate varied in quality and also in design according to the period to which they belonged, and this alone makes it desirable for a piece to have its original mounts. Unfortunately, it must be said that the majority of the walnut furniture extant has handles of a pattern dating from the late eighteenth century, or even turned wooden Victorian handles, or with modern productions. Although the modern reproduction may be more or less of the right design for the piece, they will not have been chosen with the same infallible good taste that governed the selection of the original ones. When a piece is found without the original handles, the best course to adopt is to have faithful copies made, but care should be used in determining the pattern that will be in keeping with the piece. The width of the original handle can be ascertained by measuring the distance between the old holes on the drawer front, which will have been filled up. If there is only a single hole a drop-handle is indicated. This rule, however, does not always apply, as on some pieces of furniture as many as four or five holes will be found on the drawer fronts where each handle has been fixed in turn, showing that the piece has possessed two or three sets of handles since it was first made.

Besides drawer-handles and lock-plates the hinges of cupboard doors, such as are found sometimes on a bureau-bookcase, are a type of hinge known as the " Butterfly " hinge, the " leaves " or " straps " of which are shaped and engraved. The presence of such hinges on a piece in place of the more ordinary butt hinge is a sign of good quality, which makes the

PLATE VI

(Left) A walnut chair in the style of Daniel Marot, circa 1695. *Collection of M. Harris*

(Center) A walnut chair with curved hooped back and central splat, circa 1700. *Collection of Percival D. Griffiths*

(Right) A walnut chair, circa 1685. *Collection of J. Thursby Pelham*

piece of more interest and greater value. The type of hinge that was more commonly used was one by which the door swung on a pivot formed by two pins. This "centre hinge," as it is termed, was introduced into England by the Dutch, and is often found on oak and walnut pieces; it was used in Holland throughout the eighteenth century, but is seldom found on English pieces dating later than 1725.

The screws which were used to fix the hinges and locks will be found to differ considerably from the modern screw with its accurate machine-made thread. The old screws had blunt ends, and the thread was very rough owing to it being filed by hand. The heads also varied in size.

Another point in connection with old walnut furniture which should be understood, is the effect that the shrinkage of the wood has upon it. Timber should not be used for eight or nine years after the tree has been felled, because all wood is liable to shrink. This is due to the sap drying up, which makes the wood contract across the grain therefore, a plank will shrink in width but not in length.

The effect of shrinkage on old pieces of walnut is very noticeable, as the contraction of the wood used for the carcase causes the veneer on it to split. Many walnut tables are found with a crack in the veneer across the top, and cracks are also often found in the veneer on doors of cabinets. A good example of this shrinkage of wood may be seen in the drawer bottoms of walnut pieces, when gaps will be found measuring from $\frac{1}{16}$ to $\frac{1}{4}$ of an inch between the joins of the wood. If the drawer bottoms are made in two or three pieces glued together, the contraction of the wood will open the joins; if, however, they are made in one piece, the wood will split. The same effect is also noticeable on the backs of cabinets. A further example of shrinkage is the appearance of cracks at intervals running the same way as the grain on the cross-banded mouldings of a piece of walnut furniture. The cracks in the pilasters of the bureau-bookcase (see Plate XXV) are due to shrinkage, which has also caused the join in the wood of the back to open as shown in Plate XXVI. Another example of shrinkage can be seen in the table-top illustrated (Plate XIV). It will be noticed that the sides of the two leaves where they join in the middle are concave; this is because each leaf is formed by a centre panel framed at either end by two cramp pieces, with the grain running in the opposite direction to that of the panel. The centre panel has shrunk across the grain, but the side cramps have prevented it from shrinkage along its whole length.

CHAPTER III

SPURIOUS WALNUT FURNITURE

THE amazing credulity of that section of the public that sets out to furnish houses with old furniture is the reason for the large production at the present day of spurious examples. It can truthfully be said that not half the furniture sold as antique is genuine, as it is quite impossible for the demand to be satisfied by the amount that has survived. To label a piece of furniture " antique " is to make it a saleable commodity, whereas when offered for sale as a reproduction the likelihood of finding a purchaser for it is considerably decreased. Not only is the fraudulent piece more easy to sell, but the profit realized is far greater than the legitimate profit on the sale of the modern reproduction. The fascination which the antique has for the public, and the scarcity of genuine examples, presents an irresistible temptation to the fraudulent dealer to manufacture what he cannot honestly supply.

The difference between the legitimate reproduction and the fraudulent can be clearly defined. The former is a modern replica of an old piece with no pretence to be anything other than what it appears, and is sold as such at a reasonable profit. True, it borrows from a previous age, but without disguise. The spurious piece, on the other hand, is an ingenious fraud, imitating the characteristics of a genuine piece, and made with the deliberate intention of deceiving the collector. It is sold under false pretences at an exorbitant profit ; in many cases for two or three hundred per cent in excess of its cost.

The risk to the collector of falling a victim to the vendor of spurious furniture is so great that it is essential that he should arm himself with a knowledge that will be a protection against imposition. The collector who either cannot afford the time, or has no inclination to study and acquire such knowledge, will be well advised to confine his attentions to inexpensive pieces or to reproductions ; otherwise it is more than probable he will pay very dearly for his ignorance.

There is but one way by which the collector can guard against or lessen the risk of being imposed upon, and that is to become familiar with the attributes and appearance of the genuine and untouched example. To do this a study must be made of old pieces, and by constant and careful examination in the light of his previous experience, which will be cumulative, he will gradually acquire a sound and intelligent knowledge of the salient features of genuine furniture and what it should look like.

Although a practical knowledge of this description cannot be obtained by reading, yet a book can indicate the lines along which the collector should pursue his study, and thus guide and assist his initial efforts. Soon his knowledge will enable him to understand the artistic beauty and attraction that is to be found in pieces of old furniture, and to fix in his mind a standard of excellence which will instinctively prompt him to reject the pieces that fall short of it.

In order to help the collector to recognize spurious pieces this chapter will deal with their chief characteristics, and give a brief description of the way in which they are made and the way they are faked to give them an appearance of age, and how they differ from the genuine examples.

It may be said that to disclose the methods of the furniture faker is to invite him to alter those methods and invent fresh ones, so that in a short time the information would be out of date and useless. It should be borne in mind, however, that the manufacture of faked furniture is a business enterprise. "Fakes" are commercial articles made for the purpose of trade, whilst genuine old pieces may be, and are, recognized as works of art, although when originally made they, too, were articles of commerce. The cost of labour and material obtaining to-day makes it impossible for the imitator to reproduce the old piece in anything like the same degree of perfection, except at a price that is prohibitive so far as a commercial proposition is concerned. Were this not the case, he would be able to put much better workmanship into his products and make a more faithful copy of the old work, which would be more likely to deceive. As it is, the faker is obliged to make his furniture on commercial lines to allow a good margin of profit. To show up his work, therefore, is to compel him to construct his pieces with much more accuracy and with fidelity to the original. This would call for better workmanship and for more time being spent in faking their surfaces to counterfeit the appearance of age. The increased expenditure of labour and time would add so considerably to the cost of production that it would make the venture scarcely worth his while. The more conversant collectors are with the faker's art the more proficient in his deceptions will he have to be, until a point is reached when it will scarcely pay him to produce his spurious goods.

Another point that has to be considered besides the question of the faked furniture of the future, is the danger arising from the vast quantity

PLATE VII

(Top) A walnut stool with upholstered seat, circa 1680. *Collection of J. Thursby Pelham*

(Center) A walnut stool with upholstered seat and serpentine stretcher, circa 1690. *Collection of Percival D. Griffiths*

(Bottom) A beech stool, painted black, with upholstered seat, circa 1680. *Collection of J. Thursby Pelham*

of it that has been made during the last quarter of a century, and which is still in existence. Every piece is a source of danger to the collector. The more knowledge, therefore, that he acquires, the more critical will he become of the pieces he already owns, with the result that those pieces that do not come up to his required standard of excellence, or which he discerns to be not genuine, will be discarded from his collection. It follows, therefore, that the smaller the demand for faked furniture the greater will be the demand for the genuine, and its value will increase as the former becomes less saleable.

The ways in which the faker creates his " old furniture " are many and varied, both as regards the piece which is of new construction throughout and the genuine old piece which has had its market value increased three or four times through being converted into a more elaborate and important example by the addition of spurious ornamentation. In all cases the imitator takes pains to give to his pieces an appearance of age so that the uninitiated may be more easily convinced of their genuineness. For the collector who carries in his mind a well-defined conception of what genuine furniture is like, the recognition of such pieces will present no difficulty. He will soon detect the absence of that " quality " of finish which marks the genuine piece, and miss the thoroughness of execution and the meticulous attention to detail which characterized the work of a people who belonged to an age when no consideration of time or cost of labour was allowed to restrict their art.

The greatest obstacle that the faker has to surmount is the imitating of the patina of the old piece. If he could invent a varnish which would give a colour to new walnut similar to the golden colour of the old, as it exists to-day, it would not be too much to say that in a short time he would make a fortune.

The colour of new walnut when stained and polished is brown with a slight tinge of green. The markings will not be prominent, the reason being that the wood will still contain in the soft fibre between the year rings a certain amount of sap. In an old piece the sap will have completely dried out and, in consequence, the soft fibre will be lighter in tone, making the markings more distinct and in greater contrast. The faker has to direct his efforts to do this artificially, and to entirely eradicate the green tinge caused by the sap still remaining. He proceeds to effect this by drawing out the sap and by bleaching the surface of the wood with a prepared solution of nitric acid, the destructive action of which is stopped by an alkali. This turns the wood to a lighter tone, giving more prominence to the figure. The surface of the piece is then stained slightly, and afterwards a coating of polish is applied ; it is then rubbed down with glass-paper and is again polished. After the second or third coat of polish the carving and mouldings are painted with a dark mixture of polish and colouring matter, which is done to imitate the dark parts of the carving caused through the accumulation of the dust and dirt of age, as described on page 20. This polish is wiped off from the high lights of the carving, and only allowed to remain on the more deep-cut portions. After this process has been completed, another coat of polish is applied to the entire piece, which is again rubbed down to remove the high gloss.* As a finish, the surface is thoroughly rubbed over with wax darkened by lamp black or soot, and this mixture is allowed to remain in the crevices of the carving and in the hollows of the mouldings. Gold size is mixed with the wax in order to harden it artificially, but whilst it is still in a soft state, dust and dirt are dabbed on to its surface, which form a hard crust on the wax when it dries, and materially helps to disguise the new and imitate the old piece. The faker also scatters dust and dirt in the drawers and on the carcase of the piece so as to make his deception more complete.

During the process of polishing, the surface of the piece is dented and scratched and the sharp edges sandpapered down. In order to obtain unequal indentations, say, on the top of a table, or the leg of a chair, a bunch of keys is knocked against it ; this method will leave marks and dents more closely resembling those on an old piece as they will be uneven and varied in appearance.

The more prominent parts of the carving will be burnished by a chain burnisher, which wears down the wood and gives it the smooth and worn appearance of age. The imitator generally over-does this " wearing away," as he will give the whole of the carved surface of the piece a worn appearance, removing all sharp edges ; whereas in a genuine piece the wear will be uneven, some parts being worn, whilst others will be as sharp as when they were originally cut.

The faker, to overcome the difficulty of imitating the patina, will often transfer the original veneer from a genuine walnut piece, such as a chest-with-drawers, which is in a dilapidated state and beyond repair, on to the carcase of his spurious piece. The mouldings, however, will have to be new, and with these he will have difficulty in obtaining a colour similar to the genuine veneer. In many cases they will have the greenish tinge of the new wood. This practice is usually adopted for small pieces, such as the

* As an alternative to polishing the faker will varnish the surface to give a closer resemblance to the old pieces. The dark tones in the carving, however, can only be obtained by the mixture of polish and colouring as described, for it is not possible to darken the varnish in a similar manner. Varnish is generally employed by him either for marquetry furniture, or pieces in the solid wood, as chairs with no veneered work.

cases of long-case clocks, tables, or backs and seat-rails of chairs and settees, where there are no large surfaces to be covered, as the quantity of veneer obtainable from an old piece would not be sufficient for a large article such as a china cabinet.

Besides having to imitate the patina on the exposed surfaces of a piece he has also to give the appearance of age to the unexposed parts, such as the interiors and backs of cabinets and the linings of drawers. These parts, as explained in the previous chapter, would be either of deal or oak, and the surface of the wood, never having been polished or rubbed or handled, will be in its natural state. The effect, however, of the atmosphere on both oak and deal is to darken them and give the surface a dry and mature look. To imitate this unpolished and natural appearance is far more difficult for the faker than to imitate the patina on the exterior of the piece, and to overcome this difficulty he utilises old material for the visible parts of the interior of his new piece, taking care to preserve the original surface. For instance, he will make the linings of the drawers from the oak or pine linings of the drawers of an old chest or wardrobe, which, owing to its condition, is no longer of any value. By utilizing these old drawer-linings he will have an original surface both on the outside and the inside of his new drawers, and it will only be the freshly-cut ends that will have to be stained and darkened to give the colour and appearance of age. As another example of the use of old material, the faker will make the seat-rails of spurious chairs out of the beech rails of an old four-post bed, which will have the unpolished surface and mature look of the beech rails of a genuine chair.

By utilizing this old material with its original surface the imitator gets over some of his difficulty, for he has only to fake those parts which have been freshly cut ; and these are not so important, being generally the edges of the wood and therefore less likely to be noticed. When he is reduced to using new material, he tones down the colour of the wood by acids and stains and dirties its surface so as to counterfeit the appearance of age.

To overcome the difficulty of faking the interiors of china cabinets and bookcases, the imitator paints them in oil colours, generally of a pale green or blue tint, and by rubbing dirt and colouring matter on to the painted surface and blistering and cracking it by heat, he achieves a very passable imitation of age. Paint, however, is always foreign to walnut furniture, and if it should be found on a genuine piece it must have been applied at a date subsequent to its manufacture. This, however, is of so rare an occurrence, as regards the interiors of walnut pieces, that the collector can safely assume that all cabinets and bookcases that he may come across with their interiors painted are not genuine specimens.

PLATE VIII

Collection of Percival D. Griffiths

(Top, left) A stand with octagonal top overlaid with walnut veneer; stem and tripod base of pear wood, circa 1675.

Collection of Sir William Plender, G. B. E.

(Top, right) A walnut tripod stand with tapered stem and scroll feet, circa 1695.

Collection of M. Harris

(Bottom) An oblong table with oyster shell parquetry top, decorated with lines of box-wood in geometrical design. Turned and twisted walnut legs connected by stretchers, circa 1675.

The more experienced faker invariably uses old materials as there is no difficulty in obtaining a supply of it from pieces of early nineteenth-century and Victorian furniture. He will also buy up old office fittings, which, being more or less unsaleable, can be obtained at a low cost. The use, however, of this kind of old material has its drawbacks, for there is the difficulty of hiding all the signs of the purposes for which it has been previously used. It also hampers the faker in faithfully copying an old piece which he could do if he were to use new material. For instance, he will use the pine drawer-linings of an early nineteenth-century chest-with-drawers for making the drawer-linings of a spurious Queen Anne piece ; pine, however, was never used for the carcases of drawer-linings of walnut furniture, as it only came into general use for cabinet-work in the second half of the eighteenth century. The collector, therefore, who can tell the difference between deal and pine will be armed with a good test to apply when judging such walnut pieces as he may come across, and he will view with strong suspicion all those examples that have their carcases or drawer-linings, or both, made of pine. Deal turns a light brown tone with age, whereas pine assumes a reddish tint. If a nick is made with a knife in the deal carcase of a genuine piece it will be seen that age has discoloured the wood below the surface ; if a nick is made in a piece of modern pine or deal, which has had its surface stained in order to give it a dark tone, the wood below the surface will be found to be a very light colour. This is a test which can be applied to the interior carcase of a piece when it is painted or coated with colouring matter, and is unlike the dry, clean appearance typical of the genuine example.

The imitator places pieces, over which he takes particular pains, in the sun to bleach their surfaces in order to give them a more genuine appearance. Genuine walnut furniture has an inequality of tone owing to the susceptibility of the wood to the action of light ; and so most pieces are found darker in some parts than they are in others. The imitator, therefore, places his pieces in the sun in order to obtain this unevenness of tone ; in fact if he can afford to take sufficient time over the production of his furniture, he finds the sun a valuable ally in assisting him to give it an appearance of age. The even tone of the spurious piece can be well exemplified if one of the mounts, such as a lock-plate, is removed. The colour of the wood behind it will be exactly the same as the exposed wood around it, as the faker polishes and finishes his furniture before he fixes the mounts. On a genuine piece, as already described, page 19, the unexposed wood behind the mount will be a different tone and colour from the surface of the piece which has been exposed to the atmosphere. It is not possible for him to bleach the wood around the handles and lock-plates, and at the same time to leave the wood behind them a dark tone ; but even if he could do this, it would hardly be worth his while as this discrepancy would not be discovered unless one of the mounts were removed, an unlikely procedure by an intending purchaser, unless his suspicions were aroused. The collector, therefore, as a test of those pieces which he doubts to be genuine, should remove one of the lock-plates and look to see if there is any difference between the colour and tone of the wood beneath it and the colour of the surface of the piece. A favourite trick of the imitator to give a piece a genuine look is to break or damage parts of it, which he will then proceed to carefully restore.

A defect that occurs and will assist the collector in recognizing the spurious piece is when the action of the acid with which the wood has been treated, as already described, has not been completely stopped. In such a case a white mould appears on the surface of the wood, and is especially noticeable on the unpatinated parts, such as the seat-rails of chairs ; and its effect on the exposed polished parts of a piece is to make the polish opaque and of a very light yellow colour. These peculiarities are due to the acid working out of the wood, and pieces affected in this manner entirely lose the artificial appearance of age fictitiously given to them.

Shrinkage, as described on page 37, is seldom found on spurious pieces, owing to their carcases having been made from old material which has already shrunk before being used for the second time. The collector should, therefore, always look for signs of shrinkage in a piece, such as cracks in the veneer on the tops of tables or in cabinet doors and drawer-bottoms. A sign of shrinkage on genuine pieces, that is imitated on spurious ones, is the cracks on the cross-banded mouldings as described on page 37.

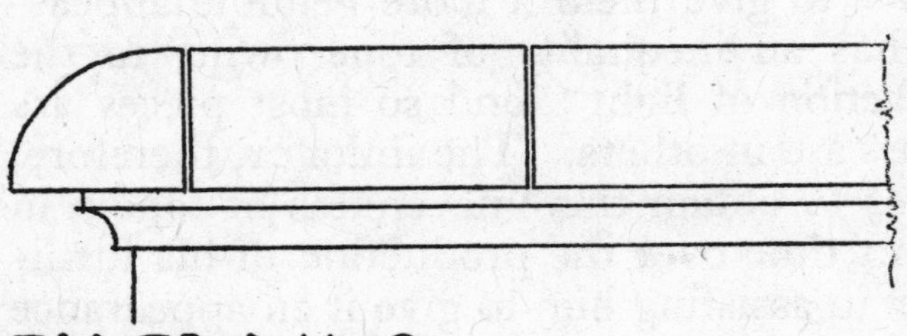

DIAGRAM 8
Appearance of cross-banded moulding showing cracks artificially made with saw.

Sometimes the imitator copies these by running a saw through the mouldings, in which case they will not be difficult to distinguish, as the cracks will all be of an equal width, and the short lengths of the mouldings formed by the cracks will be straight (see Diagram 8), and will not have the concave form caused by the wood contracting, as is the case in the genuine mouldings (see Diagram 9). Sometimes the faker will go to the trouble of damping the strip of walnut before he glues it down, and when this is done, the wood will shrink on drying, thus causing it to split in a way similar to the genuine piece.

Lakewood Memorial Library
Lakewood, N. Y.

This artificial method of shrinking, however, takes time, and therefore adds to the cost of production, and although these cracks are far more convincing than the saw cuts, the faker does not generally go to this trouble, except when making walnut picture frames, a less important undertaking than the mouldings of a piece of furniture.*

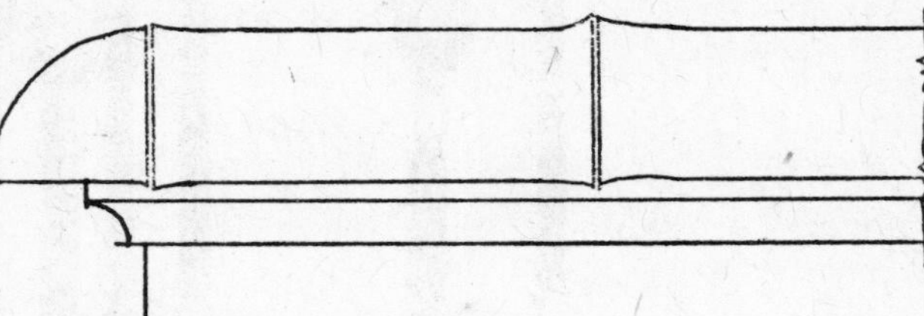

DIAGRAM 9.
Appearance of cross-banded moulding with cracks resulting from the natural shrinkage of the wood.

A test based on shrinkage can be applied to such articles as chairs, stools, settees and tables in order to determine whether they are genuine. The legs and stretchers of these pieces are morticed together, and owing to the shrinkage of the wood and the perishing of the glue, the joints give or creak a little under pressure. The newly made table or chair, the legs and stretchers of which are all tightly fixed in their mortices owing to the wood not having shrunk, betray no looseness in the morticed joints and are rigid. This test will always apply except in the case of those articles, which, owing to bad condition, have been repaired, and which in the process have had the defects caused by shrinkage corrected.

It should also be noticed that the tenons of morticed joints are held in position by pegs, and that in a genuine piece the heads of the pegs protrude slightly, which is caused by the shrinkage of the wood in which the peg has been driven. If the head of the peg is flush with the surface, it does not necessarily denote that the piece is modern, but it shows that the pegs cannot be the original ones, and that the chair or table has been taken to pieces and put together again with new pegs within recent years. This feature of the projecting pegs is not imitated by the faker; he makes them flush with the surface and sometimes, in order to save expense, he omits them altogether.

To imitate a defect very often found in old pieces that are veneered, the faker will lift and buckle the edges of the veneer by first damping it and then applying a hot iron near to its surface. He will also, when making pieces with drawers, wear down the runners by placing sand and grit between the runner on the drawer and the carcase, which, on working the drawer in and out, wears away the soft wood of the carcase. To more effectively and readily accomplish his object he will place a heavy weight in the drawers

* The faker will sometimes make these small cross-banded mouldings of a solid strip of cross-cut walnut and not go to the trouble of laying it down on a foundation of soft wood similar to the mouldings on a genuine piece, which will never be found made in this manner.

PLATE IX

Collection of J. Thursby Pelham

(Top) A walnut gate-legged table, circa 1690.

Collection of Percival D. Griffiths

(Bottom) A walnut gate-legged table with octagonal top, decorated with bands of herring-bone inlay, legs and under-framing of turned baluster design, circa 1680.

to bring more pressure to bear on the runners. The difference between the wear on the runners of a drawer caused in this manner, and the natural wear on the runners of a drawer of a genuine piece, is that in the first case more wear will show on the front part of the runner than on the back, which is due to the imitator not pulling the drawer right out, whereas, on a genuine drawer, the back of the runner will be more worn than the front, as when the drawer is pulled out the back portion of the runner on the drawer will always be in contact with the carcase, while the front portion will be free of contact. The grooves made on the bottom of the drawers by the stops fixed on the carcase should be inspected, as sometimes the imitator in making his new drawer from old material will, in using the bottom of an old drawer with the marks of the original stops on it, not place them in line with his new drawer stops. It is always very difficult for the faker to imitate artificially the wear of long use on a piece of furniture ; to do this at all well requires a great deal of patience and labour, neither of which he can afford unless he sacrifices his profit.

Pieces of walnut furniture with mouldings or carving gilded should always be viewed with suspicion, as the enrichment of these parts by gilding is a favourite trick of the imitator, not only in order to give his pieces a more decorative value, but also to assist him in giving to them an appearance of age, as he finds it far easier to fake a gilded surface than one of wood. This modern gilding has its brightness dulled by the gold being rubbed off so that the red or white ground on which the gilding is laid shows through. A thin stain or wash darkened by colouring matter is then applied and allowed to remain in the interstices and background of the carving, and dust and dirt are also rubbed into these parts to darken them. This artificial rubbing off of the gilding as a supposed sign of wear is generally too evenly executed, as old gilding will only be worn off and show the ground underneath where it has been constantly rubbed by the duster. For instance, the moulding around the panel doors of a bureau-bookcase is sometimes found gilt, and when original it will show wear on the bottom rails through being frequently dusted ; whereas, on the top-rails and styles, where it would be but seldom dusted, no wear on the gilt surface will be noticeable. The faker cannot afford time to consider what parts are likely to show wear more than others and treat them accordingly. He, therefore, gives to the whole surface a uniform appearance of wear.

The surface of genuine gilding is covered with a fine network of cracks. On spurious pieces these cracks are imitated by cutting the surface of the gilding with a sharp knife, or scratching it with a pointed instrument. On careful comparison of the genuine with the spurious piece, the difference between these marks can easily be distinguished. Another feature of

PLATE X

Collection of M. Harris

A cabinet on stand decorated with floral marquetry of various coloured woods and ivory, circa 1675. (The two centre back legs of the stand are not original.)

modern gilding is that its surface is generally soft and sticky, whereas the genuine gilding is hard and dry.

The mounts of spurious pieces also differ from the genuine mounts of the old example. As already mentioned, the original mounts were lacquered; on spurious pieces, however, the mounts are unlacquered so that the brass can be dulled and toned down to give an appearance of age. Modern handles, therefore, tarnish through exposure to the atmosphere, whereas, the old handles being lacquered are much brighter in appearance. The modern drop-handle is sometimes found with the ends of the brass strip, that in the genuine handles are pressed into the back of the drawer, fixed with small brass-headed pins. When this improved method of fixing is met with, it denotes that the drop-handle is a modern one. The nuts that fix the bolts, on the inside of the drawer-front, of the loop-handle with a back-plate, when genuine, are very unequal and rough in appearance, having been made by hand. The modern handles, made by machinery, have these nuts equal in size and of a better finish. The ends of the bolts on the old handles are tapered to a point, whereas the modern bolts are cut off square and not tapered. The back-plates of the modern mounts are generally thicker than old ones; this refers, however, to the modern hand-made handle, and not to those stamped out by machinery, which are generally thin and much more accurate in the shaping. The modern handle fits tightly in the slots of the bolts, whereas the old handles work easily and freely owing to wear. On a piece with its original drop-handles it will be seen that where the end of the handle touches the drawer-front there is a semicircular mark (Plate VIII*c*). The imitation of this on the spurious piece, although it will not be forgotten by the imitator, will not have the same convincing appearance, as he will not trouble to spend the necessary time in perfecting these slight and subtle signs of wear. On an original piece, say, of a cabinet door or the flap of a bureau, there is very often found a number of small indentations under the keyhole, caused by opening the lock with a key on a bunch, which has scratched and dented the surface of the wood just below the keyhole. Many other instances of the signs of wear on genuine pieces could be given.

Besides pieces of new construction made out of old and new materials, plain walnut pieces are enhanced in value 300 or 400 per cent by enriching them with decoration. This is accomplished by inlaying their surfaces, or by the addition of carving; the former method will be dealt with more fully in Chapter V on Marquetry Furniture. The carved decoration is usually confined to enriching the backs of plain settees and chairs with shallow carved ornament which is glued on to the top of the existing veneer in a manner similar to the old examples, as described on page 34. This method of giving value to a plain piece is, however, more usually found in eighteenth-century mahogany chairs and settees, of which there are far more examples than walnut. Mahogany, being a darker wood, is also better adapted to this deceit than the lighter coloured walnut, as it is easier to make the new carving look convincing.

An ingenious fraud which is sometimes carried out in the case of chairs is that by which a set of three or four genuine chairs is converted into a set of six—a much more saleable number. If three new chairs were made, the difference between them and the old ones would be too noticeable, especially if the old and new chairs were examined side by side. The three old chairs, therefore, are taken to pieces and exactly the same quantity of new parts made. When the chairs are assembled, the old and new parts are amalgamated so that each chair of the set of six has some parts that are old and some that are modern. For instance, each chair might have one genuine front and back leg, two old seat-rails, and either a new cresting with a genuine splat, or an old cresting with a modern splat. By this intermingling of old and new parts the deception is much harder to discern, especially when the intending purchaser is told that one or two of the chairs have been " slightly restored."

The difference between the marks made by hand tools and modern wood-working machinery may also afford convincing evidence of the genuine or spurious character of a piece. In the age of walnut furniture only hand tools were available ; but the imitator frequently employs, for the sake of speed and economy, machine tools that leave distinctive marks upon the wood and so bear witness of modern workmanship. In the past the rough cutting of the timber was done with a pit-saw, the marks left by it being uneven and straight, but not always parallel, and the saw marks of the smaller hand-saw are similar, though finer and more even. The modern mechanical circular-saw leaves regular curved and parallel marks across the grain ; and with the band-saw the marks are vertical, always parallel and close together. These machine saw-marks in a crude form, can generally be seen on modern packing-cases where the wood has been left in a rough state and not " cleaned off."

The imitator would not leave such saw marks on the exposed surfaces of a piece, but they are difficult to eradicate, and he will rarely go to the trouble and expense of wholly removing them from parts not generally seen, such as the framework of upholstered chairs, the undersides of stretchers and the insides of seat-rails, and also from the interior of the carcase of a piece.

In the same way the machine plane will leave distinctive marks on the surface of the wood, so that its use can be detected. The hand-plane takes off long thin shavings, leaving the surface smooth and even ; the machine-plane works with a scooping action which flicks off shavings about $\frac{3}{8}$ inch in length, leaving very slight regular and parallel indentations along the surface. These hollows are not easily perceptible, but if the wood is viewed at an angle, with the light striking sideways along its surface, the " waves " can usually be seen, and they are always more apparent after the piece has been stained and polished.

The mouldings, too, on an old piece, were worked by hand with various planes for the different members, and will be found to vary considerably in section at different points in their length. A template of the profile at one end of a hand-made moulding, when passed along its length, will fail to fit in a number of places. This irregularity is absent in those turned out by a moulding machine which again leaves regular indentations along the surface. These marks of machine tools can only be removed by a lengthy and tedious process of rubbing down with glass-paper ; but the faker rarely spends the time to do this properly as it makes too serious an inroad into his profit.

The old veneer is found in thicknesses varying from $\frac{1}{16}$ inch to $\frac{1}{8}$ inch, and was cut by hand with a pit-saw. The cutting is said to have been done by special workmen, who travelled from place to place visiting workshops once or twice during the year ; and the cabinet-makers reserved for these visits the selected pieces of wood from which they desired the veneer to be cut. The thickness of the modern veneer is about $\frac{1}{24}$ inch to $\frac{1}{16}$ inch, and it is cut with the machine circular-saw.

It must be realized that just as there are degrees of quality in genuine pieces of furniture, so there is a variation in the quality of faked examples. Roughly, there are two markets for faked furniture, and the demand of each is supplied by two distinct types, the skilled artist and the commercial faker. The former, whose work is ambitious and whose reward is considerable, aims at deceiving and entrapping the collector and the connoisseur. He pits his brain and skill against the knowledge and experience of the expert. The limit of his endeavour, therefore, is fixed by the knowledge which is common to them both. For this reason he will not make a Queen Anne cheval glass, because such a thing never existed, and he knows that the connoisseur is fully aware of this fact. Neither will he make a walnut china cabinet, because to manufacture such a piece with sufficient accuracy to deceive the knowledgeable collector would necessitate so much labour and entail so great an outlay that the profit would be negligible. His attention, therefore, is concentrated on faking furniture which leaves as little room as possible for the discovery of his methods and tricks, and which at the same time, if genuine, would command a considerable price in the

PLATE XI

Collection of M. Harris

A cabinet or wardrobe of architectural design decorated with floral marquetry of various coloured woods, circa 1680. (This piece is said to have been made for James II when Duke of York.)

market. He therefore confines his attention to the production of such articles as chairs and settees, of which genuine examples are both rare and costly, but which from their design require very little expenditure of either labour or material. For instance, in the case of a chair or settee with the back, seat and arms upholstered, the legs and under-framing exposed to view would alone need the faker's manipulation. The consequent low cost of the production of such pieces allows him to spend more time in perfecting them. He buys plain undecorated pieces, the value of which he considerably enhances, as already described, by introducing carved or inlaid ornamentation. Another of his efforts is to reconstruct parts of genuine pieces and transform them into something more valuable and more saleable.

The commercial faker, on the other hand, caters for a larger and less critical market, and is responsible for most of the fakes that are made. His is an organized trade run on commercial lines, and based on the ignorance and gullability of his customers. As opposed to the specializing efforts of the master faker, who makes comparatively few pieces for selected patrons at high prices, the commercial faker makes a large quantity and sells them at an extortionate profit, though not at a price which they would command were they genuine. The skilled faker, when successful, obtains the full value of the genuine piece which he has counterfeited. The commercial faker floods the market with spurious walnut china cabinets, imitations of rare writing tables, small bureaux and early card tables inlaid with marquetry, all of which he makes as attractive as possible, and generally of a small size suitable for modern requirements.

The design of these pieces is based on that of the rarest and most sought-after examples of walnut furniture. He excels in the manufacture of china cabinets, sometimes on a stand with turned legs connected by stretchers, sometimes with cupboards below. He gilds the mouldings and carving to enrich their appearance, which also simplifies his work, and invariably colours the interiors with oil paint, as has been previously pointed out. They are described as genuine examples of the rare William and Mary furniture, and are sold at a price wholely disproportionate to the cost of their production. In order to make his pieces more saleable the faker gives them an elaborate form, but having no genuine examples to follow, their proportion is bad, and their design but seldom true to the period to which they are supposed to belong, the desire to increase their selling possibilities outweighing any consideration for artistic truth.

The bad proportion and design of a faked piece are sufficient in themselves to betray it to the trained eye. Whereas, the old cabinet-makers quietly pursued their vocation on traditional lines slightly varied to suit the current fashion, the modern commercial faker to please his untutored clients does not scruple to break the canons of taste by designing and making a piece of furniture whose basic idea is borrowed from a bygone age, but which he fondly believes is improved by his innovations. For instance, he will make a small cabinet to suit the needs of his customers, with the domed top of a design borrowed from a bureau-bookcase, and he will mount it on a stand, the legs and stretchers of which he will copy from a rare William and Mary table, and he will decorate its surface with panels of marquetry. This hybrid, ill-proportioned cabinet will, consequently, be the creation of his own fancy, a hotch-potch of borrowing and adaptation, with no real likeness to any piece which existed at the time to which he will unblushingly claim that his fake belongs.

From the foregoing description of the activities of the imitator, it can be realized to what length the imitation of old furniture is carried at the present day.

The collector, after a short time spent in studying genuine examples will not find it very difficult to be able to distinguish the pieces of the commercial faker. They all bear the same hall-mark. Their surfaces are coated with polish and colouring matter which hides and obscures the wood and its figure. The colour is generally a muddy brown or yellow, sometimes with a greenish tinge, and there is a soft waxy feel, sticky to the touch, very unlike the hard, dry and smooth surface of an original piece. If these spurious pieces are seen in strong daylight or sunlight the semi-opaque coatings of polish on the surface of the wood can be seen distinctly. A similar examination of a genuine piece with a good patina will show that the polish or varnish on its surface is clear and transparent, not obscuring the figure of the wood in any way. When possible, pieces should be examined in daylight, as in artificial light this false patina is less noticeable. Any variation in the colour of a piece caused through modern additions or restorations can be more easily detected in daylight, as any new work will always vary in colour and surface condition from the original parts. For instance, if a new leg has been added to a chair, however well the restoration has been carried out, it will not be possible, either by bleaching, staining or polishing the wood, to give it exactly the same appearance. Besides making a rule of examining furniture in daylight, the collector should invariably make a point of closely examining the unexposed parts of a piece, for if he is doubtful about the genuineness of the patina on the polished parts, he is sure to find conclusive evidence on the unpolished portions to prove whether the piece is genuine or not.

To distinguish a spurious piece by the skilled faker will require a much greater understanding of old pieces, as it will not be the piece of new construction that the collector has to fear so much as the old carcase reconstructed or veneered with old walnut veneer, and a plain piece newly decorated with carving or marquetry inlay. But here again, he will find " patina " and " quality " are his greatest safeguards.

If the collector, as already suggested, forms a standard in his mind of those pieces that he buys, and adheres to the golden rule of forming his judgment of a piece on what he sees and not on what he hears, he will find it not as difficult to recognize the genuine piece as he did when he lacked a definite standard to work upon. The collector should remember that it is better to buy a perfect piece even at a high price than an imperfect one at a low price ; if he does not buy the former he is sure to regret it ; but he is much more certain to regret it if he buys the latter.

CHAPTER IV

STUART WALNUT FURNITURE

1660–1702

ALTHOUGH in France and the Low Countries during the sixteenth century walnut was the wood generally employed for making the better class of furniture, it was but rarely used in England at that period. Long after the vogue for walnut had been established on the Continent, the English remained faithful to oak; and it was not until the beginning of the reign of Charles II that walnut wood was used to any extent for furniture in this country. This apparent reluctance on the part of the English craftsman to abandon the use of oak was primarily due to the scarcity of walnut wood in England during the reign of the Tudors, for it was not until Elizabeth's time that walnut trees were introduced and planted in any quantity.

Some writers, however, contend that a great deal of walnut furniture of English make was in existence at the end of the sixteenth century; and that in fact all the best English pieces of that time were made of this wood; the assumption being based on the fact that a considerable quantity of "walnut-tree" furniture is referred to in contemporary inventories of certain late Elizabethan houses.

It has been pointed out that English furniture of the late seventeenth century, although to a large extent influenced by contemporary furniture of the Low Countries, always preserved its native characteristics, and this is even more true of English furniture during the Elizabethan epoch, for all the surviving oak furniture of that time has a distinctly indigenous cast, and differs in the handling and treatment of the carving and the quality of the workmanship, from contemporary foreign examples. The difference noticeable in the carving shows the Flemish work to be more carefully and skilfully rendered than it is in the best English work, which is treated in a broader and bolder manner, both as regards its design and execution. The individuality of the English piece can always be detected by the trained eye, and however great may be the similarity to a foreign piece it is this distinctive character of the English example that is certain to denote its provenience.

Included amongst the quantity of Elizabethan furniture that has survived are a few pieces made in walnut wood, and as these examples do not vary, either in design, treatment, or workmanship, from their contemporary prototypes in oak, and bear, also, the same English individuality, they may, without doubt, be properly designated as of English manufacture. These examples, owing to the scarcity of walnut wood in England, may have been made from foreign walnut, especially in view of the fact that foreign oak was being imported at this period for the wainscotting in the best houses, English oak being much coarser in grain and more difficult to work than the Continental varieties. This certainly is true of several of these rare pieces of walnut, the wood being foreign and not English. These walnut examples are, however, so few in number compared with the large number of far more important examples in oak, that they form no criterion for the assumption that English walnut furniture was made in Elizabeth's reign to the extent that has been suggested.

For the enumeration of so much walnut furniture in certain late sixteenth-century inventories we shall find a valid explanation in the swarms of foreign craftsmen brought over by Henry VII and Henry VIII from France, Italy, Burgundy and Flanders to erect the new royal palaces of Sheen, Molesey and Nonsuch; and in their subsequent employment on the new palatial homes built by the Tudor nobles in emulation of their royal masters. The employment of foreign craftsmen was prevalent during the sixteenth century, and even as late as the first decade of the seventeenth century we find that Janivere, a French or Flemish woodworker, was making the wainscotting, chimneypieces, and other elaborate woodwork for Hatfield House. This and similar woodwork which has survived in a number of other contemporary houses in England, is distinctly foreign in character as regards its design and execution, the carving being of a very high quality and markedly superior to any contemporary English work. It is improbable, therefore, that the English noble, who went to the length of employing and bringing over foreign workmen, to carry out the elaborate structural decorations of his house, would be content to entrust to the native craftsman the making of the more important furniture for its adornment. The present-day scarcity of English walnut furniture of the late sixteenth century, and the fact that these Elizabethan inventories relate to houses for the building of which foreign craftsmen are definitely known to have been employed, points to the conclusion that the walnut furniture in such houses was either the work of alien hands in this country, or that it was imported from abroad.

That practically nothing now remains of this supposed wealth of English Elizabethan walnut furniture is hardly to be explained by the

PLATE XII

Collection of M. Harris

A writing-cabinet with fall-down front decorated with floral marquetry of coloured woods, circa 1695.

suggestion that walnut wood is more perishable than oak, in view of the quantity of contemporary French and Flemish walnut furniture extant. Probably more of it exists than is suspected, but it is now recognized as of foreign make and classified accordingly. Of such examples, known by existing records to have been made in this country, may be cited the pieces at Hardwick Hall, which are French in design and execution, and can be attributed to the foreign craftsmen employed by Bess of Hardwick on the various houses erected by her.

It is significant that if walnut wood was ever adopted by the English cabinet-maker for furniture in the late sixteenth century, as is contended, it had but a fugitive vogue with no continuing tradition, its use dying out completely for the greater part of the seventeenth century, from the early years of James I to the Restoration, and that this cessation in its use coincided with the rise of English architects and craftsmen, and the consequent disappearance of the imported foreign workmen. It cannot, therefore, be considered inaccurate to assign the beginning of the English walnut period to 1660.

The return of Charles II after the Commonwealth Interregnum meant not only the restoration of the Monarchy, but of the art life of the people. It must be remembered that the ordered progression by which the fashionable taste in furniture had spread from the Court, who were arbiters of taste and dispensers of fashion, down, through the nobility, to the houses of the middle and lower classes, was broken by the Civil War and the suppression of the Monarchy which had sent both the king and his followers into exile. During their involuntary sojourn abroad they had ample opportunity to appreciate the higher scale of domestic taste and comfort that they found on the Continent, and they returned with new ideas and standards of luxury for the refurnishing of their old homes. The change in English furniture brought about by this new incursion of foreign ideas was revolutionary, altering the material of which it was made from oak to walnut, breaking the continuity of the design and, as already described, affecting the methods of its construction.

The two important foreign influences that brought about this change were those of the Dutch and the French. Of these the stronger was that of the Dutch, to whom the English craftsman, lacking a creative power of his own, had generally turned for inspiration, not only during the Elizabethan period, as has been seen, but also in the time of the Commonwealth, when the plain and simple lines of the furniture were adapted from contemporary Dutch examples.

The new vogue in furniture was fostered by the growth of luxury among the upper classes, who copied the costly fashions of the Court; so that early in the walnut period upholstered furniture, hitherto confined

PLATE XIII

Collection of Percival D. Griffiths

A mirror in frame with hood, decorated with floral design marquetry in various colour and stained woods. The cross-banded mouldings to the frame are of olive wood, circa 1680.

to the homes of the great nobles, had made an appearance in the houses of the well-to-do. The furniture of the middle and lower classes continued to be made in oak or fruit-wood, but its design gradually became affected by the new dispensation, so that at the beginning of the eighteenth century the oak furniture of even the provincial districts was following the lines of the walnut.

The Revocation of the Edict of Nantes, by Louis XIV, in 1685, and the consequent exodus of the Huguenots from France to the neighbouring countries of England, Holland and Germany, also, indirectly, left its imprint on the design of English furniture. Many of these French immigrants were craftsmen, architects, designers and artists, and their art, imbued with the traditions of the School of design of Louis-Quatorze, was of so distinct a character that it was termed in these countries of refuge, "*le style refugié*."

The accession of William and Mary to the English throne gave a fresh impetus to the Dutch influence, for the new king was not only a Dutchman by birth, but always maintained his predilection for the men and Arts of his native country. A foreigner at his accession, he remained one until his death. He had cold and repellent manners, combined with a gift of silence in the seven languages of which he was master ; but his more human instincts seemed to have found expression in a delight for the arts of architecture and decoration, of which he left concrete evidence in additions to Hampton Court Palace, and in the new palace that he built at Kensington. For these notable works he employed Sir Christopher Wren as architect, but the interior decoration and furnishing were mainly entrusted to one, Daniel Marot.

Marot came of a family of French artists and craftsmen. Born about the middle of the seventeenth century, he was a pupil of Le Pautre, one of the originators of the Louis-Quatorze School of design. A Protestant, he took refuge in Holland in 1685, and entered the service of William of Orange, accompanying his Royal Master to England on the latter's accession to the English throne four years later. He was one of the chief exponents of "*le style refugié*," and, although his work was strongly reminiscent of the French style, it was modified by the Dutch environment in the early years of his involuntary exile.

William III made Marot his Minister of Works, in which position his talents were mainly devoted to designing the interiors of rooms, which would include the chimneypieces, wainscotting, furniture and hangings. He also turned his attention to iron-work, gold and silver plate and garden architecture. His principal work in England was confined to that on which he was employed by the King, but it is more than probable that he received commissions from other wealthy clients for the decoration and furnishing

PLATE XIV

Collection of Sir William Plender, G. B. E.

A writing-table with folding top (illustrated above), decorated with seaweed marquetry in panels. The two front centre legs swing forward to support the hinged leaf of the top, circa 1695.

of their houses, and that he became the dictator and leader of fashionable taste during William's reign.

Little of the furniture actually designed by Marot now remains, apart from the beds, mirrors and a few remaining stools and chairs at Hampton Court Palace ; but his influence on the design of English furniture of the William and Mary period and later is distinctly traceable in many of the pieces that have come down to us. The fusion of the Louis-Quatorze and Dutch styles, that we owe to Marot, endowed such English pieces with a richness of design and decorative value, that, despite their foreign feeling, give them a distinctive character.

Under separate headings, the various articles of Stuart walnut furniture up to the end of the reign of William III are dealt with, in order to familiarize the collector with the genuine types he is likely to meet with to-day.

As already mentioned walnut tables are rare, but chairs of this half of the walnut period have survived in greater number than any other article of furniture ; and there are many examples of such articles as cabinets and chest-with-drawers, but these are mostly in marquetry, or decorated with oyster-shell parquetry. In fact, most of the veneered furniture surviving from this first half of the period is decorated in either of these two methods, and the plain walnut examples belong mainly to the second half, which is treated in Chapter VI, to which the reader is also referred for particulars of articles first made in this early part of the period, but of which examples are more generally found, to-day, dating from 1700 onwards. As marquetry furniture is dealt with separately in Chapter V, the marquetry examples of the first half of the period are only briefly mentioned in the following notes.

Chairs, Stools, Daybeds and Couches

The chairs provide the earliest examples of walnut furniture, both in regard to the use of wood, and also the transition in design from the simple Cromwellian furniture to the more elaborate and decorative style of the reign of Charles II. From surviving examples it has been possible to trace a gradual evolution and unbroken continuity of design from the decade preceding the Restoration until the death of William III, and to follow various changes in form and detail as new motives were first introduced. By these transitional steps the typical features at various dates can be roughly classified as in the table given on the next page ; but it must be remembered that, with the great variety of detail, typical features of two or three different dates may be found on one chair, in which case its approximate date will be that of the latest feature.

PLATE XV

Collection of S. E. Prestige

(Left) A long-case clock with carcase of oak veneered with ebony and decorated with panels. Eight-day striking movement by Ahasuerus Fromanteel. Height, 6 feet, 5 inches, circa 1670.

(Center) A long-case clock with carcase of oak veneered with oyster-shell parquetry inlaid with stars. Eight-day striking movement by Thomas Tompion. Height, 6 feet, 6 inches, circa 1675.

(Right) A long-case clock with carcase of oak veneered with ebony and decorated with panels. Mounts of brass, water gilt. Month movement by Joseph Knibb. Height, 6 feet, 11 inches, circa 1695.

Table Showing Changes in Design of Chairs from 1650–1700

	Approx. date of introduction	Typical Features
(1)	1650–60.	Low oblong back; spiral-twist rails, legs and stretchers. Similar in form to the "Cromwellian" chairs. The ball turning, typical of the latter, often found combined with the spiral-twist turning typical of the Carolean period. This type of chair is sometimes in walnut, but more often in beech or oak.
(2)	1660.	Spiral-twist rails, legs and stretchers. Coarse cane panel in seat and back. Back higher and squarer in shape, see Plate II (*a*).
(3)	1663.	Similar chair to (2), but cresting to back deeper and decorated with rosettes and foliage, and sometimes with crown.
(4)	1665.	Similar to (3), but with carved front stretcher, generally similar to design of cresting, instead of spiral-twist stretcher, see Plate II (*b*).
(5)	1667.	Similar chair to (4), but with cresting of back and front stretcher decorated with amorini, supporting a crown. Side-rails to the cane panel in back decorated with carving, see Plate III (*b*). The carving in this type more finished, in higher relief and pierced.
(6)	1670.	Front legs have become scrolled, and the cresting of back, front stretcher and side-rails to cane panel decorated with "S" shaped scrolls.
(7)	1670.	Legs, stretchers and rails of turned baluster design in place of former spiral-twist, see Plate III (*c*).
(8)	1675.	Chairs with upholstered backs and seats having scroll legs and "S" shaped scrolls to front stretcher. Back of chair made higher. Sometimes these chairs were made with padded wings to the back, being the forerunner of the winged arm-chair.
(9)	1675.	Chair with upholstered seat, but back decorated with carved wooden splats instead of cane panel. Chairs also made of beech, painted black.
(10)	1685.	Chair with elaborately carved and pierced wooden back, upholstered seat on turned cupped legs connected by serpentine stretchers centred by a turned finial, see Plate IV (*c*).

	Approx. date of introduction	Typical Features
(11)	1685.	Chair with cresting to back supported on top of the uprights instead of between them. Back of chair made narrower. This type of chair found with back and seat filled with fine-mesh panels of cane (Plate IV (*b*)), and also with carved splat back and upholstered seat similar to (10).
(12)	1695.	Chair after the style of Daniel Marot, cabriole front legs, connected by stretchers and ending in scroll feet. Fine-mesh caning in back; upholstered seat, see Plate VI (*a*).
(13)	1700.	Chair with curved or fiddle-shaped back having one centre splat carved and pierced. Cabriole front legs connected by stretchers and ending in scroll feet or *pied-de-biche*, see Plate VI (*b*).

The changes of design indicated in the above table apply not only to the chairs and daybeds, but also to the underframing and legs of stools and couches, and cover the general run of all these articles at the approximate dates given.

The chairs, originally, were made in sets comprising, probably, two arm-chairs and six or twelve single chairs, as a far larger number of the latter are found to-day. Arm-chairs must also have been made in sets of six or more, as several of such sets have survived.

Single chairs are met with in pairs, but more frequently as solitary examples; and the arm-chairs are nearly always found singly, to meet with two or more of the same design being very unusual. From the quantity of chairs existing which have spiral-twist rails, and stretchers decorated with amorini supporting a crown, they would appear to have been made in large numbers. Of the other varieties, those with upholstered backs and seats, or with carved splats in the backs and upholstered seats, are both rarer to-day than the earlier examples with cane panels. The most valuable chairs, however, are those with the elaborately carved backs, and those in the style of Daniel Marot. An arm-chair in the Marot taste is a great rarity, in fact, judging from its present scarcity, it could have been but seldom made. Pairs of the single chair are not uncommon, and sets of four or six are sometimes met with, but these sets are undoubtedly relics of larger sets extending to a dozen or more.

To add to the comfort of chairs with cane seats they were usually fitted with loose upholstered squabs. For the upholstered types of Carolean chair, damask and figured velvets were used for the coverings, which were further enriched by a trimming of deep, tassel fringe. Damask and velvet were also employed for the William and Mary chairs; but, in this period, needlework coverings, so popular from the next reign onwards, were sometimes used. The original upholstery fabrics are seldom found on chairs to-day, but at Knole a number of specimens are preserved with their contemporary coverings of damask and Genoese velvet.

A type of upholstered chair first introduced in the time of Charles II was the arm-chair with wings, and this variety has continued in favour up to the present day. The early Charles II and William and Mary examples are extremely rare, and were made with very high backs and boldly shaped wings and arms.

Of the various stools of the period the early type had a cane seat, but examples of it are seldom met with. The stool with upholstered seat, dating from 1675, was originally made in sets numbering, perhaps, six, twelve or more. Another type of the upholstered stool has six legs instead of four; this long variety, however, is only known by a few surviving examples. A few have also survived with eight legs instead of six, and are more in the nature of a long upholstered seat. These long seats or stools are confined to-day to historical mansions in which they have remained since the day they were made, such as the few specimens to be seen at Hampton Court Palace. The circular stool is another type of this period, and an example is shown in Plate XVII (*c*). Stools in the style of Daniel Marot are of great rarity, and although a number must have been made, few have survived.

In addition to these chairs and stools in walnut, examples have survived of elm, chestnut and beech, the latter usually painted black.

These articles will also be met with in oak, but the hardness of this wood made it less suitable for the elaborate carving, and it was, in consequence, seldom employed.

The earlier type of Charles II daybed is that with a cresting to the back decorated with rosettes and a crown, and these early specimens have, on the two long sides, spiral-twist rails, which, about 1665, were superseded by carved stretchers, thus following out the design of the contemporary chairs. Some of these latter daybeds have the carved stretchers on one side only, this economy being adopted, presumably, when the daybed was intended to stand against a wall. Daybeds of about 1685, like the chairs, have the cresting of the back supported on the uprights, and the backs and seats are filled with fine mesh panels of cane. Daybeds of a design of a later date than this do not appear to have survived, and the last variety, which is the rarest of all, has eight legs instead of six.

The back of the daybed was invariably made to hinge so that it could

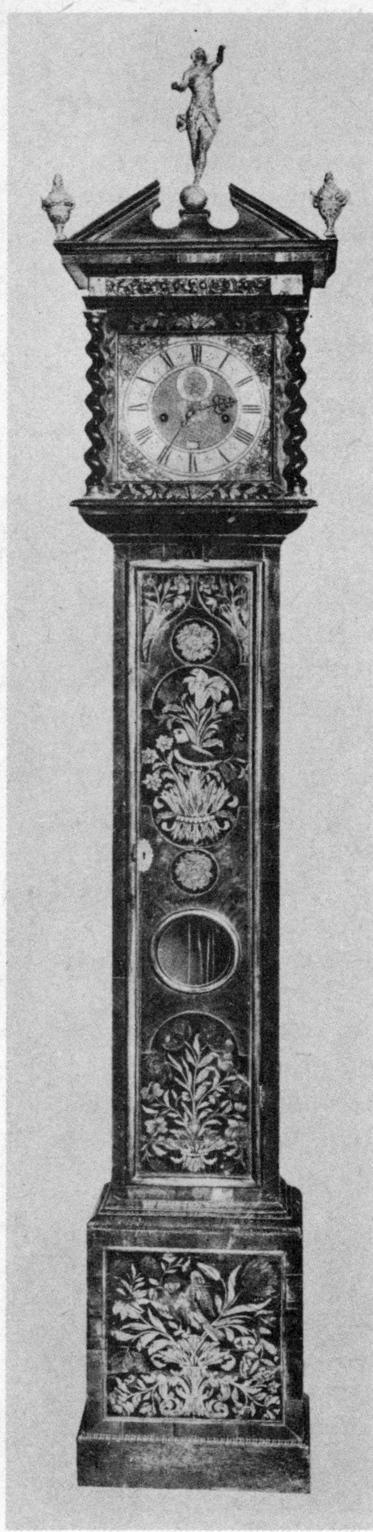

PLATE XVI

Collection of Sir John Prestige

(Left) A long-case clock with carcase of oak decorated with floral marquetry of various coloured woods in panels. Month striking movement by Philip Corderoy. Height, 7 feet, 6 inches, circa 1685.

Collection of S. E. Prestige

(Center) A long-case clock with carcase of oak, decorated with arabesque marquetry. Eight-day striking movement by Jeremiah Newbrough. Height 6 feet, 10 inches, circa 1705.

Collection of S. E. Prestige

(Right) A long-case clock with carcase of oak overlaid with straight-cut walnut veneer. Eight-day striking movement by Benj. Gray and Just. Vulliamy. Height, 7 feet, 7 inches, circa 1750.

be raised or lowered by cords. Examples are sometimes found with two backs, one at each end ; these are much rarer and more highly prized to-day than those with the single back. Another variety of the daybed, of which a few examples are extant, has an upholstered seat and back and eight legs, but in this type the back was not adjustable. These upholstered daybeds appear to have been made up to the end of Queen Anne's reign, from which period most of the surviving examples date.

The high-back upholstered couch, the earliest specimens of which date from about 1675, is another piece of Stuart furniture which is of great rarity. In form these couches are like two arm-chairs placed side by side with the centre arms removed ; the legs and stretchers and arm supports, which are the only parts in wood showing, following out the design of the contemporary chairs. These couches were invariably made with the backs, seats and arms upholstered, as an example with a wooden back is not recorded ; although one or two very rare couches are extant with the upholstering of the backs framed in by a carved wooden rail. Such an example of the William and Mary period has survived of dimensions equal to three arm-chairs, and designed with legs and stretchers accordingly.

Painted Beech Furniture

Chairs and stools of beech, painted black, have already been referred to, and from the number of such articles found to-day, they appear to have been made in very large numbers during the first half of the walnut period.

This is all the more evident because beech, of all timbers used for furniture, is the most liable to attack by the worm, to the ravages of which many of the surviving pieces bear witness ; and it follows, that those which have come down to us can only be a tithe of the number originally made.

The reason for the manufacture of this furniture in beech is somewhat obscure. Beech has always been plentiful in England, and it is reasonable to suppose that furniture could be made of it at less cost than the fashionable walnut, to meet the demand of the less wealthy members of society of the late seventeenth century. Another explanation for this quantity of beech furniture was the scarcity of walnut wood in England at the time, so that beech was used as a suitable substitute in districts where the walnut was not obtainable. This type of painted beech furniture appears to have been first made about 1675, as the earlier Carolean chair, with spiral-twist turning and amorini, does not appear to have been made in beech, no example being recorded. The design of nearly all the beech chairs extant is that with turned-baluster supports and stretchers and scroll front legs. This beech furniture appears to have gone out of fashion by about 1695,

PLATE XVII

(Top, left) A walnut stool, circa 1715. *Collection of Percival D. Griffiths*

(Top, right) A walnut stool, circa 1735. *Collection of Percival D. Griffiths*

(Bottom, left) A circular walnut stool, circa 1695. *Collection of Sir William Plender, G. B. E.*

(Bottom, right) An oval walnut stool, circa 1715. *Collection of Percival D. Griffiths*

as the surviving examples, in point of design, do not appear to be of a later date. Chairs of an elaborate nature, such as those with carved splats in the backs, were not made in beech, these more costly and high-quality examples being reserved for walnut.

The reason for ceasing to make the beech furniture at this date may have been due to the importation of foreign walnut into England to meet the demand for walnut furniture, there being, therefore, no necessity to use beech as a substitute.

Both single and arm-chairs have survived to-day, the former generally being of the variety with the narrow high back and small cane seat. Examples of stools and also of the early winged arm-chair in painted beech are more frequently met with than their prototypes in walnut, which are to-day exceedingly scarce, especially as regards the winged arm-chair.

The use of beech appears to have been confined mainly to chairs and stools, as a beech daybed or couch does not, so far, appear to have come to light. Tables were undoubtedly made in painted beech, as a few have survived ; and it is more than probable that a number of other articles were made in this wood although not to the same extent as the chairs and stools.

On a few of these beech chairs and stools the carving has been enriched with gilding, but an example treated in this manner is seldom met with. Besides these partially-gilt pieces, a few suites, consisting of chairs and stools, made in beech, have survived, with their legs, stretchers and arms entirely gilt, and their backs and seats upholstered.

The reason why this furniture was painted black, instead of being left in the natural wood and polished or varnished, is very difficult to account for, especially as a number of examples, mostly chairs, are extant treated in the latter way. Owing to their scarcity to-day in comparison to the painted examples, it is evident that it was the more general custom to paint this furniture instead of polishing it.

The painted beech furniture to-day is, by no means, so valuable as the walnut, because the painted surface not only lacks the bronze-like patina of the latter, but the sharpness of the carving is lost under the thickness of the paint. It has also a rather shabby look, the paint in many cases having become blistered and cracked ; and on the prominent parts of a chair, such as the arm or the top of the cresting, where it has been rubbed or handled, the paint will be worn away, disclosing the wood underneath. This last peculiarity rather enhances than mars its effect, besides being a sign that the piece is genuine, and has not been repainted within recent years.

In some cases the paint has been removed and the wood stained and polished to imitate walnut, but this is never satisfactory, it being impossible

PLATE XVIII

Collection of Sir William Plender, G. B. E.

(Left) A walnut barber's chair with four cabriole legs, knees of front legs decorated with shell, circa 1720.

Collection of Percival D. Griffiths

(Right) A wing chair with walnut cabriole legs. Original gros point upholstery. Back raises and lowers by a rachet, circa 1715.

to remove all traces of the black paint from the grain of the wood and the interstices of the carving. Pieces so treated are invariably muddy in colour and the surface condition new and raw in appearance.

Present Condition and Spurious Imitations

The collector who wishes to acquire specimens of Stuart walnut chairs will find numbers of genuine examples to choose from ; but he should make a point of confining his purchases to examples of good quality and patina. The former is specially noticeable in the execution of the carving, which on some will be coarse, whilst on others it will be finely wrought and more elaborate in design. This does not refer, however, to the earlier examples dating before 1665, which, as already mentioned, were cruder and coarser in execution than the later types.

The patina of these Stuart chairs, stools and daybeds will be found of varying quality. On examples with good patina the walnut will have a highly-polished bronze-like appearance, the projecting portions of the carving being light in comparison with the parts in low relief, which are of a dark tone caused through the accumulation of dust and beeswax. It would appear, judging from surviving examples of this Stuart walnut furniture, that it was the custom to finish their surfaces not with polish, but with a coat of thin transparent varnish. Unfortunately a number have been coated with a thick opaque varnish, which differs very considerably from the original transparent variety, and has been applied most probably in the past for the purpose of renovation. Fortunately, the majority of these chairs, stools and daybeds have escaped depreciation at the hands of the French polisher, owing perhaps to the difficulty of successfully applying the polish on their carved stretchers and turned rails.

The question of the amount of restoration that these articles have received naturally affects their present-day value ; the following notes, therefore, on the condition in which they are likely to be found by the collector, and, also, on the types which are frequently copied by the imitator to-day, may be found useful in arriving at a proper understanding of these pieces.

Most genuine chairs of the type with the cane backs and seats will have had the caning renewed, particularly that of the seats ; the seat-rails will also often be found in a more or less restored state, but these necessary renewals do not decrease the value of an example to any great extent. The original caning can be recognized by its brittleness and the coarseness in the strands, which will be loose from wear. The modern caning will have finer and more pliable strands, and the new cane panels, which will be toned down with stain to give them an appearance of age, will be tightly stretched and unyielding.

The part of a genuine chair that is most likely to have been restored is the front stretcher, owing to its exposed position and consequent liability to damage ; and this defect will be found in both arm and single chairs, especially the former. As the design of these stretchers in most chairs corresponds with that of the cresting surmounting the back, the designing of a new stretcher presents no great difficulty to the imitator. This restoration depreciates the value of a chair, and special care should be taken to see whether there is any variation in the surface condition and colour of the wood of the front stretcher from the other parts of the chair. The piercings of the carving on both sides of the stretcher and the surface of the back should also be examined, as on an original stretcher the wood should be perfectly hard and smooth to the touch, due to long exposure to the air and deposits of dirt and wax from use and domestic polishing. In the modern imitations the piercings of the carving will be rough, and the surface condition sticky from the recent application of polish and coloured wax to give an antique appearance. The crevices of the carving should also be scrutinized for traces of dark-coloured polish which will have been applied as described on page 42 ; and the presence of new glue at the ends of the stretcher where it joins the legs should also arouse suspicion. To properly insert the tenons of the new stretcher into the mortice holes of the legs, the chair should be taken to pieces ; but the imitator rarely goes to this trouble, and by stretching or wedging the front legs of the chair apart as far as possible, will " spring " the new stretcher into its place. It is impossible to do this with tenons which accurately fill the mortice holes, so one or both tenons are, consequently, cut away, and the spaces left in the mortices are filled in with wedges to keep the stretcher firm and in position. It is not possible for the imitator to make his new stretcher so perfect that it cannot be detected by careful scrutiny.

Many of the Stuart arm-chairs will be found with a modern arm. The collector, to detect this restoration, should look for any variation in the shape or finish of the two arms, or in their surface condition and colour. The undersides of the arms should be also examined, for such parts, being hidden from view, the imitator will not usually go to the trouble of faking. The underside of a new arm will in consequence show signs of recent manufacture in comparison with a genuine one.

Many fraudulent copies of Stuart walnut chairs, especially those with upholstered back and seat, are to be met with ; and the various tests given in Chapter III should be applied for their detection, especially the one regarding shrinkage in the mortice joints, which causes the chair to creak and give a little under pressure. All genuine chairs of the Stuart period, even if they have been restored, should respond to this test, and not be found rigid and unyielding. Another point in connection with the mortice joints of genuine Stuart chairs is the slight projection of the heads of the pegs, as described on page 47. It is practically impossible for the imitator to get the right colour and surface condition on the ends of new pegs, as, being cut across the grain, it is difficult to stain them to the requisite colour.

Besides fraudulent sets of chairs the imitator also makes daybeds and couches, especially the latter, with the high upholstered back, turned legs and serpentine or carved stretchers.

The imitator also turns his attention to making examples of these chairs, stools and couches in painted beech. In fact he prefers to work in this wood, as it is much easier to obtain an appearance of age on a painted surface than on one of polished walnut. He has made many spurious examples of the Charles II circular beech stool, also of the winged arm-chair with the high upholstered back, turned-baluster legs and rails, and an elaborately carved front stretcher. In making these beech imitations old material, obtained generally from Victorian beech bed-rails, is used. As has already been mentioned genuine beech furniture is invariably found to-day affected by the worm, and there are few genuine examples that do not show some traces of its ravages more particularly at the base of chair legs, which in many cases have been eaten away. Beech examples which are free from worm-holes should be viewed by the collector with suspicion, although the imitator, knowing this defect in his pieces, will sometimes remedy it by making artificial ones with a drill. Artificial worm-holes made in this manner, however, bear no relation to the condition of the wood inside, as in a genuine leg affected by the worm, the whole of the leg will become honeycombed with passages which will be filled with dust. The worm disliking the polish and glue, will, instead of coming out on the surface, continue to make burrows in the interior. As long as the outer surface of the leg is unbroken it will preserve some stability, but with the outer crust of the wood removed, the dust gradually filters down the borings and out of the external breach until the leg becomes a mere shell, which crumbles or collapses under strain or pressure. Worm-eaten wood when badly affected sounds hollow if tapped.

The collector in order to detect these spurious examples of chairs, stools,* daybeds and couches both in beech and walnut, should not fail to examine the unpolished seat-rails of these articles. The wood of the rails should have, as already described, a dry mature look, be smooth to the touch and not sticky, nor exhibit any signs of bleaching with acids or

* A number of spurious stools have been made out of the front legs of two single chairs. Some are found with upholstered seats, but a favourite type to be made in this manner is the early stool with the cane seat.

PLATE XIX

Collection of C. D. Rotch

(Left) A walnut chair with back and seat-rail overlaid with burr walnut veneer, and with unusual moulded seat rail and carved apron piece, circa 1725.

Collection of Percival D. Griffiths

(Right) A walnut arm-chair, with back and seat rail overlaid with burr walnut veneer, on to which has been applied carved decoration in low relief, circa 1725.

staining. On the genuine beech chairs and stools these parts are left unpainted; the imitator, however, in order to overcome the difficulty of giving them an appearance of age, paints their surfaces similar to the exposed parts. A feature of a genuine walnut or beech stool, which the imitator is not able to copy, is the patination of the inside seat-rails caused by the hand gripping them when the stool is moved. In the corners of the rails against the legs, where the fingers will not reach, the wood will be light in comparison with the handled parts midway between the legs. This feature can be better realized by comparing the undersides of the rails of a stool with those of a chair, which, being lifted by the back, will not have the rails patinated as described.

In all upholstered furniture the number of tack marks on the framework and seat-rails may have some bearing on the genuine or spurious character of the piece, although it would be necessary to open up the existing upholstery to see these marks. If the chair or stool frame is seen stripped of its upholstery prior to the latter being renewed, it is well to take note of these tack marks, as, if few in number, there may be a suspicion that the piece is not as old as it purports to be. The presence of old sacking and webbing on the underside of an upholstered seat should not be regarded as a sign of genuineness, as the imitator can obtain plenty of such old material, which he invariably uses for the upholstery of his fraudulent pieces to give them a more convincing air of antiquity.

Attention has already been directed to the similarity between English furniture of the first half of the walnut period and the contemporary Dutch furniture. This is specially marked in the case of chairs, as in contemporary Dutch pictures walnut chairs are shown of nearly identical design to the English ones. The spiral-twist turning of the English chair differs, however, from that on the Dutch example, the English spiral-twist having the rope small and the hollow large, whereas the foreign twist has the hollow small and rope large. This difference can be more readily appreciated by reference to the accompanying diagram, No. 10.

DIAGRAM 10.
English &. Foreign spiral twist turning

The Dutch also favoured oval panels of cane in the backs of their chairs, whereas the English chairs had oblong panels. This rule is not invariable, but the percentage of foreign chairs with oval cane panels is much greater than with the English ones. There are, too, a much larger

PLATE XX

(Left) A walnut arm-chair with upholstered seat and back, covered with gros and petit point needlework, circa 1735. *Collection of Percival D. Griffiths*

(Right) A walnut writing-chair upholstered with the original gros and petit point needlework covering, circa 1720. *Collection of Frank Partridge*

number of foreign chairs with upholstered backs and seats than English examples.

In addition to the Dutch chairs contemporary Italian and Spanish examples in walnut will be met with in England, mainly importations into this country in recent years to meet the demand for walnut furniture. They generally have upholstered backs and seats with a turned rail in front in place of the carved stretcher. This type with the turned-baluster front stretcher is but seldom found on English chairs. As shown on the table at the beginning of this chapter a spiral-twist front stretcher was in favour up to 1665, when it was superseded by the carved stretcher. The Italian examples of these chairs and stools are, generally, very light in colour owing to the walnut fading in the sunny clime of Italy. Foreign stools with turned rails, instead of the carved stretchers, are also met with. The collector should be able to recognize these types of foreign chairs and stools in order to avoid acquiring them in mistake for English examples, their value being considerably less.

Some French and Dutch walnut chairs of a design contemporary with the William and Mary period are met with in this country. These foreign examples are of a more elaborate design than the English chairs, some having cane panels in the backs and some elaborately carved splats. A favourite *motif* of design, often met with in the backs of these foreign examples, is a Roman head in a medallion ; this feature is never found on an English chair. These highly ornamented Dutch and French examples, unlike the plain foreign specimens mentioned above, are as valuable to-day as the contemporary English chairs, although they err on the side of over-elaboration, and lack the good taste of the more restrained English design.

Tables

The only Stuart walnut table of which any number has survived is the oblong table with veneered top on spiral-twist or baluster legs, similar to example, Plate VIII (*c*). The earliest of these tables does not appear to date before 1670, and the majority of them have four legs, but larger examples with five legs, similar to the one illustrated, will sometimes be met with. A drawer is invariably fitted in front, whilst the back is sometimes veneered, but more often left with the carcase disclosed, denoting that this type of table was originally intended to stand against the wall. The earlier examples have the spiral-twist legs connected by flat veneered stretchers. These were followed, as in the case of chairs and other leg furniture, by the baluster-turned legs. This type was in turn succeeded by the turned-cupped leg. A few tables dating from the end of Charles the Second's reign have the rare scroll leg with the serpentine stretcher (see Diagram 11); but very few examples with these legs are extant.

This table with the spiral-twist legs is generally found to-day decorated with oyster-shell parquetry of laburnum wood, sometimes of olive; and a number of examples will also be met with in marquetry. The later tables with the turned-cupped legs are usually decorated with the straight-cut walnut veneer sometimes formed into panels with inlaid lines of box-wood. The legs of these tables were more often made of elm or fruit-wood than walnut; and, in good quality examples, the front edges as well as the tops of the flat stretchers will be found veneered. In most tables, however, the front edge of the stretcher will be left unveneered like the back edge, these edges being formed by the deal foundation.

DIAGRAM 11.
Scroll leg as found on tables & cabinet stands.
Circa 1680 to 1700

A number of tables of this type will be met with in fruit-wood, oak or elm; these tables, being made in the solid wood with no veneer, could be produced at a lower cost and were made for a cheaper market. Many of them are of a later date than the design of the legs and stretchers would appear to indicate, for the reason that they were copies made in country districts of the expensive and fashionable veneered tables of a decade or two previous.

The present-day condition of these tables shows them in varying states of repair. Generally the veneer of the top is either imperfect or blistered and raised, and the stretchers broken or lost; the last fate may also apply to the legs. These parts should accordingly be examined by the collector to determine how much the value of the table has been lessened by restoration. Many genuine examples will also have been depreciated by French polishing, whilst others will be coated with a thick varnish; these tables, having the figure of the wood thus obscured, have lost their decorative value. Spurious imitations of this table are usually confined to examples in marquetry, and these will be dealt with in the next chapter.

Judging from the quantity of these tables that has survived they are the only type that could have been made in any number up to the end of the reign of William III. The gate-legged table, as already mentioned, is but rarely found in walnut, and this is remarkable considering that from 1660–1700 it must have been the most usual form of domestic table, as so large a number of examples in oak are extant. The genuine walnut gate-legged table, when found, is generally of small dimensions, similar to Plate IX (*a* and *b*). A few larger tables have survived, but these usually have their tops of oak or elm with their legs and stretchers only of walnut. Probably the extravagance of using large planks of walnut for the tops of such tables may be a reason why so few were made of this wood; and although this difficulty could have been overcome by veneering the top, it would be necessary, to prevent the foundation warping, to veneer both sides, which would have added considerably to the cost. It is only by reviewing the technical difficulties that a possible solution of the inexplicable scarcity of walnut gate-legged tables can be found. The majority of small gate-legged tables extant are either of oak or fruit-wood, such as pear, large tables not being possible in the fruit-woods, owing to the small size of the planks obtainable from these trees.

Another Carolean walnut table is that with the folding top, similar to the marquetry example shown in Plate XIV. This type of table is found with spiral-twist, baluster, turned-cupped or tapered legs (as example illustrated), according to the date when it was made.

A variation of this table, also found in walnut, is that with a hinged leaf, which instead of folding over on to the top, lets down similarly to the gate-legged table. Fewer examples of this type of table are extant than the one with the folding top.

The collector who wishes to acquire a genuine walnut table of this period, unless very fortunate in his search, will have to confine his purchases to the oblong type with drawer, as the other varieties he will be less likely to meet with.

The earliest walnut table made for the purpose of card playing would appear to be the one already described with folding top, as a few examples have survived with their tops covered with velvet. Another form of card table with a circular top was introduced in the reign of William III, and was supported on tapered legs connected by stretchers, as shown in example, Plate XXXI (*a*). The top of the table when closed was semicircular in shape, half the top being hinged, and this, when opened to the full circle, was supported on two of the back legs that pulled out after the manner of the gate-legged table. Small drawers were generally fitted in the freize of the table under the top. The collector who is desirous of purchasing such a table will find great difficulty in doing so, although the imitations of the commercial faker abound.

PLATE XXI

Collection of Percival D. Griffiths

A walnut settee, with the rare feature of masks decorating the seat rail, circa 1715.

Writing-Cabinets, Bureaux, and Writing-Tables

Pieces of domestic furniture designed specially for writing purposes were first made in this period. The earliest forms were the cabinet with fall-down front (see Plate XII) and the bureau-on-legs.

In the writing-cabinet with fall-down front the lower part was composed of a chest-with-drawers,* as in the example shown. This piece was of typical Continental design, and its introduction into this country was prior to that of the bureau-on-legs, but whereas its popularity in England lasted only until about 1715, the same form of writing-cabinet continued to be made in Holland and France throughout the eighteenth century. The earliest examples of this cabinet, which would date about 1675, are usually found decorated with oyster-shell parquetry or marquetry. These parquetry and marquetry specimens are, however, much rarer than the examples in walnut, which are by no means rare to-day, many having survived both in the burr and the straight-cut walnut. It is, moreover, not a piece that is very highly valued, owing perhaps to its rather square and heavy design, and its unsuitability for writing purposes.

The bureau-on-legs had two gates, similar in construction to those of the gate-legged table, for the support of the fall-down front, which, when opened, formed a surface for writing, and disclosed an interior fitted with small drawers and pigeon-holes for letters and papers. This design of a bureau was undoubtedly introduced from Holland, and the earliest examples do not appear to be of a date prior to 1680. The surviving specimens of this early bureau have either plain baluster-turned legs or the tapered and cupped legs of the William and Mary period, connected by stretchers of square section. This early type of bureau-on-legs is extremely rare to-day, and the majority of those extant are in the straight-cut walnut veneer, whilst two or three examples are known decorated in marquetry.

That neither of the above articles are recorded as made in oak or fruit-wood points to the fact that they were pieces of furniture made for the houses of the wealthy and educated people, and not for the poorer classes, who would have no use for such articles.

The bureau-on-legs was soon followed by the bureau mounted on a base with drawers, and the earliest examples of this type, judging from their design, would seem to have been made about 1690. With this piece the fall is supported by runners which are pulled out from the carcase. Contemporary with the bureau-on-drawers was the bureau-bookcase, which

* A few rare examples of this writing-cabinet mounted on stands with spiral-twist legs, connected by flat veneered stretchers, are extant.

was the bureau-on-drawers with the addition of a bookcase surmounting it; but as most of these bureaux and bureau-bookcases date from 1700 onwards they will be dealt with in Chapter VI on the furniture of the second half of the walnut period. In this chapter will also be mentioned two other forms of writing-tables which were not introduced until the closing years of the seventeenth century. One is the small bureau-on-stand, similar to examples, Plate XXVII (*a* and *b*), and is another variation of the bureau; the other is a form of writing-secretaire with knee-hole and let-down front similar to example, Plate XXXVI (*a*).

The above articles of furniture were those introduced into England for writing purposes up to the death of William III, although there are other forms of writing-tables* which have survived from this period; notably one supported on scroll legs which is at Kensington Palace, said to have been used by William III, and another marquetry table at Windsor Castle, made for him, which is a copy of a contemporary Louis XIV example. These rare examples cannot, however, be said to be typical pieces of this period.

Genuine examples of bureaux, secretaires, and writing-tables of the first half of the walnut period, with the exception of the secretaire with fall-down front, will be seldom met with to-day; and, unfortunately, many of the examples that have survived have had their patina destroyed by French polish. The attractiveness of the design of the early bureau-on-legs to the collector, and its suitability for writing purposes, has caused the commercial imitator to make many spurious examples, for which he finds a ready sale. These imitations are generally designed with spiral-twist legs, a type of leg which it is doubtful would ever be found on the genuine example, as it had declined in favour before the introduction of this bureau into England. The great scarcity of genuine examples of this bureau should make the collector suspicious of those that he meets with, in view of the abundance of spurious ones existing. Besides the bureau-on-legs the imitator also copies the small bureau-on-stand, as this is another decorative and readily saleable piece of the walnut period.

Cabinets, China Cabinets and Bookcases

The cabinet of the first half of the walnut period, of which any considerable number survive, is that with the solid doors enclosing a number of small drawers around a central cupboard. These cabinets were made mounted on stands, having either spiral-twist, baluster or scroll legs,

* The table with folding top, similar to example in marquetry (Plate XIV), was also a table used for writing at this period.

connected by flat veneered stretchers, whilst others were mounted on a base composed of drawers. They would appear to have been first made about 1670, and to have remained in favour until the end of William the Third's reign, after which date their popularity waned and they were superseded by the lacquer cabinet. They are but seldom found in the straight-cut walnut veneer, being decorated generally either with oyster-shell parquetry or with marquetry.

Larger cabinets of this type were also made on stands with five or six legs instead of four, similar to the example in marquetry, Plate X. Those with six legs generally have shelves in the interior, instead of the small drawers and central cupboard.

Many of the smaller type, originally mounted on stands, are found to-day with the stands missing. In fact, this is generally the case, for while a surprising number have survived, considering the early period from which they date, only a few possess their original stands, the slender legs of the latter having, in most cases, been broken down by the weight of the cabinet. The collector who wishes to purchase a cabinet of this description should investigate the stand carefully, as within recent years a large number of these cabinets have had the missing stands renewed. The stand most frequently copied is that with the spiral-twist legs, and to recognize a spurious example particular examination should be made of the flat stretchers. The imitator will use old material for the foundation of these stretchers, as by so doing he will preserve the original surface on the underside. The top and front edge of the stretcher he will cover with old or new veneer, but the back edge, which on an original stretcher will be left unveneered, has a freshly cut surface which must be faked to give it an appearance of age. In the majority of cases the imitator will avoid this difficulty by veneering the back edge. This would never be found on the genuine stretcher.

The cabinet with small drawers in the interior was a much more favoured piece of furniture at this period than the walnut bookcase or china cabinet with shelves and a glazed front, as such pieces, dating from the time of Charles II to William III, are practically unknown to-day, only very few specimens having survived.

To account for the scarcity of bookcases with glazed fronts, it must be remembered how few books there were in the average household of even the wealthy classes ; and that in the libraries of the large mansions of this time, books were housed in fitted bookcases, which were not separate articles of furniture, but built in with the wainscotting of the rooms. Although Queen Mary possessed the china cabinets specially made for her by Gerreit Johnson, and other wealthy people may have had similar cabinets, yet the number that were made at this period could only have been

PLATE XXII

Collection of M. Harris

A two-chair-back walnut settee. Front legs cabriole and terminating in lion-paw feet, circa 1735.

negligible, otherwise many more would have survived the vicissitudes of time. From the second half of the walnut period we have inherited a plain type of cabinet or bookcase which will be referred to in a later chapter.

The demand of unwary collectors for walnut china cabinets has led to the making of so many spurious examples, that, if they were genuine survivals of the William and Mary period, it would imply not only that the china cabinet was one of the most popular articles of furniture at that time, but that hardly a household in the country was without one. This ready sale for china cabinets has also resulted in the importation of a number of Dutch examples, as the making of such cabinets in Holland, especially during the first half of the eighteenth century, does not appear to have been so restricted as in England. These Dutch china cabinets have the fronts glazed with oblong panels of glass, and in some examples, the sides were canted and also glazed. They are mounted on stands with turned or tapered legs connected by flat stretchers, or on a base with drawers. Usually they are of large dimensions, being 6 or 7 feet in width, and have a curved and shaped top, generally ornamented with coarse carving. These foreign cabinets, which have no counterpart in English furniture, will be found in walnut veneer and oak, whilst others will be decorated with coarse floral marquetry. The interiors were often painted; this, as already noted, was an expedient never employed by the English cabinet-maker.

Chests-with-Drawers and Chests-on-Stands

The earliest chest-with-drawers, like the cabinets, would appear to date from about 1670, and from this time up to 1685 the majority of the surviving examples are decorated with oyster-shell parquetry or with marquetry. Examples in walnut do not appear to have been much in favour before 1685, hardly any having survived. These early chests-with-drawers generally measure about 3 feet to 3 feet 6 inches in width, and have five drawers, two small and three long.

The above remarks concerning the chests-with-drawers also refer to the chests-with-drawers on stand. From about 1670–1685 the stands were low and were invariably designed with a shallow drawer, with three spiral-twist legs in front and two behind, connected by flat veneered stretchers, which were sometimes shaped. By about 1685 the design of the stand altered, having four legs in front instead of three, of the tapered or turned-cupped design, typical of the William and Mary furniture. These later chests-on-stands were higher than the early ones, and are found to-day in veneered walnut. The tops, being above the eye-level,

PLATE XXIII

Collection of Percival D. Griffiths

(Top) A two-chair-back walnut settee. Arms terminating in eagles' heads, circa 1715.

Collection of M. Harris

(Bottom) A walnut side table with legs of unusual design, circa 1720.

were not veneered* as in the lower and earlier examples, but finished with a cornice.

All these chests dating up to about 1695 will have the wide dovetail of Dutch appearance, similar to Diagram 2, also the half-round cross-banded moulding on the carcase round the drawer fronts, similar to Diagram 4.

In Chapter V will be mentioned the examples decorated with marquetry, and in Chapter VI the further development of this article in the second half of the walnut period will be traced.

The stands of these chests, like those of the cabinets, are usually found to-day imperfect, with the legs and stretchers missing, and the chest and the upper part of the stand, containing the shallow drawer, resting on the floor. Examples met with on complete stands should be scrutinized carefully to see whether the latter are modern restorations. The remarks on page 81 concerning the veneer on the edges of the stretchers will apply also to these stands.

Tripod Stands

In the earlier part of the walnut period the tripod foot as a support for tables was first introduced into England. The earliest example of a piece with this foot that survives to-day is a type of stand, similar to Plate VIII (*a*). The tops were generally octagonal in shape, and were of deal overlaid with walnut veneer. The stem has spiral-twist turning, similar to the example shown, and, together with the scroll feet, was, occasionally, made in walnut, but more generally of elm or fruit-wood. About 1690 the stem became tapered, similar to the small table illustrated, Plate VIII (*b*). All these early types of tripod stand are very Dutch in feeling, and a number of Dutch examples, sometimes decorated with coarse floral marquetry, with the tapered stem, will be met with in this country. The English examples, similar to those illustrated, are much rarer.

This type of walnut stand has received considerable attention from the imitator, and he has made a number of fraudulent examples of the early type with the spiral-twist stem. The collector should, therefore, in his search for a genuine specimen, realize its rarity, and view with suspicion all those that he encounters.

The development of this tripod stand and table in the second half of the walnut period will be dealt with later, as after its introduction into England it became a very popular type of support for candlestands, tables,

* Some transitional chests-on-stands will be found with the four legs in front and with the veneered top.

PLATE XXIV

Collection of Percival D. Griffiths

A bureau bookcase overlaid with burr walnut veneer, with the unusual feature of the doors in upper part being glazed with bevelled glass. Lower part with knee-hole and cupboard instead of drawers, circa 1725.

and fire-screens. The tripod design persisted throughout the eighteenth century, undergoing various changes in treatment according to the current ruling fashions.

Bedsteads

The massive oak bedsteads of the preceding periods were undoubtedly used, and continued to be made, though of lighter design, in the first half of the walnut period. In Court circles in the time of Charles II, the oak bedstead was supplanted by the upholstered bed, which was a later development of the earlier examples of this type that was first introduced into England in the reign of James I, such as the upholstered beds at Knole.

This bed, which was of the four-post variety, had no woodwork visible with the exception of the feet of the posts. The cornice, posts, and head-board had the upholstering fabric, generally of velvet or damask,* stretched and pasted over them, and the valances and curtains were trimmed with heavy fringe and galon. The curtains at the foot hung round and hid from view the posts, which were plain, tapered and round in section, not being a decorative feature as in the oak bedsteads.

In the reign of William III this upholstered State bedstead became more elaborate in character, and the height was increased to be proportionate to the taller rooms then in vogue. This development of the more elaborate and ornate bedstead was due in great measure to Daniel Marot, who was especially happy in his designs for upholstered work. Many of his published designs for bedsteads show great elaboration of detail, both in the hangings and in the elaborately carved and moulded cornices and head-boards.

The four corners of the tester top were sometimes surmounted by plumes of ostrich feathers, whilst on other examples turned or carved vase-shaped finials covered with the upholstering fabric will be found. The hangings of the bedstead would be similar to the curtains of the room, the valances to the window-curtains being surmounted by a covered cornice similar in design to those of the bedstead.

Practically the only bedsteads of the first half of the walnut period of which examples still exist are the State and Royal beds, similar to those preserved at Hampton Court Palace, and in other historical mansions, where they were reserved for the use of Royal and distinguished guests.

This type of upholstered bedstead, however, set the fashion, and,

* Bedsteads of this period also had their hangings of needlework. Some examples, extant, are of a very elaborate nature, the making of which must have involved considerable time and labour.

towards the end of the century, smaller and less elaborate examples had begun to make their appearance in the houses of the wealthy. That so few specimens of these simpler upholstered beds are extant may be due to their destruction in the eighteenth century, when they became shabby or were superseded by the mahogany bedsteads, which, judging by the number of posts that have survived, must have been made in considerable numbers.

The further development of this upholstered bed in the second half of the walnut period will be shown in Chapter VI.

CHAPTER V

MARQUETRY FURNITURE

1670–1720

MARQUETRY in this period was a decoration entirely in veneer, in which a design carried out in one or more coloured woods was inlaid into a background formed of another wood of a different colour. It differed from the marquetry of the Elizabethan age, which was not an inlay of veneers, but the inlay of a wood into a solid background.

The veneered marquetry had no period of evolution or transition in England ; it was a Dutch craft brought into this country in a fully developed state. The earliest pieces of furniture decorated with it would appear from their design to have been made about 1670,* and as already commented upon, the marquetry examples, made from this date to about 1690, have survived in far larger numbers than those veneered with the plain walnut, with the exception of pieces of oyster-shell parquetry, which method of decoration was as much in favour between these dates as marquetry. It might be deduced from this predominance of furniture decorated with marquetry and oyster-shell parquetry over that in the plain walnut veneer that the last-named did not come much into vogue before William III ascended the throne. Such an assumption, based on the rarity of the plain walnut examples of a date prior to this, may, however, be erroneous ; and the survival in larger numbers of marquetry and parquetry pieces be attributable to the greater care and attention bestowed by past owners in appreciation of their more elaborate and decorative character. The theory that marquetry was of earlier date than the plain walnut, however, is supported by the fact that the former, being far more expensive to produce, was confined, on its introduction into England, to the patronage of the wealthy

* Samuel Pepys writes in his Diary for the year 1664 about a visit he paid to the house in Lincoln's Inn Fields of Mr. Povy, M.P., Treasurer for Tangier, where he saw one of the rooms floored with woods of several colours, " Like the best cabinet work I ever saw." This undoubtedly shows that the new fashion of inlaying woods was in vogue as early as 1664, and it is possible that furniture decorated with marquetry was made about this date, although from the design of surviving examples, none would appear to be so early.

classes, the less costly furniture in plain walnut making its appearance later to meet the demand of those not so well endowed. This is consistent with the evidence we possess in the examples surviving to-day, although it is impossible of proof; and, unfortunately, in the absence of authentic information in contemporary literature or records, the reasons underlying changes of fashion in the furniture of the past can only be surmised. No effort of imagination is required to realize the rich and gay effect of the marquetry furniture when new; that it became very fashionable amongst the rich of that day is amply proved by the number of examples that have survived.

The design of the early marquetry which was copied from the Dutch was floral, depicting flowers in vases with birds. At first, it was confined in panels (see Plate X), but later the panels were discarded, and the marquetry was designed to cover the whole surface (see Plate XI). Floral marquetry in the last decade of the seventeenth century lost the strong Dutch influence of the earlier examples, the pattern being less sparse and the design more elaborate, sometimes exhibiting cupids and acanthus leaf scrolls amidst the flowers, a change attributable to the influence of Daniel Marot and his school of design.

In the reign of William III two other varieties of marquetry, known as the seaweed and the arabesque, made their appearance. The former, as the name denotes, has a pattern representing the flowing floral lines of seaweed. It also resembles the finer leaves of the endive plant, and is, occasionally, therefore, called "Endive Marquetry." The arabesque variety was inspired by the brass and tortoise-shell designs of the French cabinet-maker, André Boule. A variant of the arabesque design is known as the "Persian," owing to the resemblance it bears to a pattern peculiar to the Persian carpet.

Seaweed marquetry is generally found in panels, whereas, in the arabesque, the pattern is of the "all-over" type, and covers the whole surface. The seaweed type is more characteristically English than any of the other varieties, to all of which it is markedly superior, not only by reason of its restrained design, but on account of its greater decorative value. It supplies another instance of how the Englishman, having assimilated a foreign art, evolved his own interpretation of it, ultimately discarding what was not in consonance with his native taste. Seaweed marquetry went out of vogue in the first decade of the eighteenth century. The arabesque was the last phase of English marquetry, which declined in favour and became decadent by the end of Queen Anne's reign, but lingered on until 1720.

In all types of English marquetry the pattern was usually formed by inlaying light-coloured woods into a darker background of walnut or other dark-coloured woods, such as coromandel or lignum vitæ. The inlaying of dark-coloured woods into a lighter background was seldom resorted to, as by this arrangement the marquetry lost in decorative value. The woods used for the pattern in the floral marquetry were many, and from examples which are extant to-day, native woods that were plentiful would seem to have been commonly employed. Such woods were holly, apple, pear, sycamore, and yew. Bog oak and beech were also used. For the flowers natural coloured woods were chosen, such as orange, citron and red sanders or sandalwood.

To add still further touches of colour to the floral marquetry and also to make it more realistic, the leaves of the flowers were dyed green. To give more emphasis to the pattern, the walnut background was sometimes stained to a black tone which, to-day, through exposure to the light, has faded to a rich dark brown. Ivory* was often employed for the petals of the smaller flowers, and also for the leaves, the latter being dyed a bright green.†

In the seaweed and arabesque marquetry, holly and box were generally chosen for the pattern, but, for the early floral marquetry, box was not often used, probably owing to its scarcity in this country. The reserves between the marquetry panels were sometimes filled with straight-cut walnut veneer, but in higher-quality examples these spaces would be decorated with oyster-shell parquetry, generally of laburnum wood.

In making panels of marquetry, the design was first drawn out on thin tough paper ; and to make the necessary copies of it, the lines of the original drawing were afterwards pricked through. The design thus perforated, was fastened down over another sheet of paper and a fine, coloured powder dusted over its surface, the dust penetrating the perforations and leaving an imprint of the pattern on the undersheet. Further copies were made in the same way as required.

In the seaweed and arabesque varieties, where only two woods were used, one for the background and one for the pattern, two layers of veneer, one of a dark wood for the background and the other light for the pattern, were fixed together by glueing each on to a sheet of paper placed between them. The paper design was then pasted on to one side of these two veneers, and the marquetry cutter, guided by the lines on the design, proceeded with a fine saw to cut the pattern out of both sheets of veneer at one operation, after which the two layers were separated with a thin knife blade, splitting

* Bone, as a substitute for ivory, will not be found on old English marquetry furniture, being unsuitable, as, having an " open grain," polish and dirt would tend to discolour it.

† The holly or box veneer was stained green in the sheet before it was cut. Ivory was, however, stained after it had been cut and glued on to the carcase of the piece.

PLATE XXV

Collection of Captain W. F. Dickinson

A narrow bureau writing-cabinet of unusual design, overlaid with burr walnut veneer, supported on short cabriole legs, and claw and ball feet. Carved cornice and pediment and capitals of limewood and gilt. The door panel pilasters fitted with bevelled mirror, circa 1735.

(Piece is of exceptional quality and preservation. Carcase of English oak and the drawer linings of walnut. This latter is unusual and is seldom found in large drawers of walnut pieces.)

the interleaved paper in two. It will be realized that the pattern had been cut out of both sheets; and that in the light wood was then fitted into the pattern spaces cut out of the dark wood forming the background. A piece of paper was then glued over the surface to hold the two together preparatory to the panel being glued on to the carcase of the piece of furniture.

With the floral marquetry, where several different coloured woods were used in the design for the various flowers and birds, a different method had to be pursued. In this case the various portions of the design were cut separately from each other and from the background. For each flower, bird, or other ornament, a "packet" of veneers of coloured woods would be glued together as already described; the number of veneers in each packet being determined by the different coloured woods required. The patterns for various flowers, birds, and other ornaments were then cut out separately from prints of the design and pasted on to their respective packets of veneer. After the cutting of each packet the portions of the various veneers required in the design were placed in trays, preparatory to their being fitted into each other and into the background.

The veins of leaves or the petals of a flower, when made out of one layer of veneer, were produced by saw-cuts, which were filled up with dark coloured wax to accentuate them. For instance, the bases of the vase on the doors of the cabinet, Plate X, are each formed from one piece of box. The gadroon moulding and acanthus foliage are delineated by saw-cuts in the veneer. This introduction of detail by means of the saw is typical of old English marquetry. Engraving or etching the surface, instead of cutting the veneer, was never employed at this period; although in the late eighteenth century the inlaid work of the Adam or Sheraton Schools was treated in this manner.

It is characteristic of floral marquetry that the pattern is never repeated, although the balance of effect is maintained. In arabesque or seaweed marquetry of poor quality a panel will have both sides exactly symmetrical. On such a piece one-half of the pattern only would need to be cut in double layers of veneer, and these on being folded out formed the complete panel. By this method half the time and labour was saved in cutting the veneer and, also, in making the design. Sometimes a quarter of a panel was cut in eight layers of veneer, four for the pattern and four for the background, and these quarters when laid together made the complete panel. This labour-saving method of producing marquetry panels was seldom employed by the old marquetry cutters; and when met with, to-day, is generally found on clock-cases decorated with late arabesque marquetry.

The old marquetry cutter rarely utilized the "contra" or reverse

PLATE XXVI

Interior of the top part and bureau of the writing-cabinet illustated, Plate XXV.

veneers that were left over from the cutting of the seaweed or arabesque patterns. These produce a marquetry with a dark pattern on a light background; and such marquetry, when genuine, is usually found decorating pieces of a late date, when the art of the marquetry cutter was in its decadency.

A method by which the light colour of the box or holly could be shaded so as to give depth to the pattern was by scorching the surface of these veneers. This was effected by placing the small pieces of veneer, or so much of them as required shading, in hot sand, and by this expedient the shading could be graduated in tone.

After the veneering of the carcase with the marquetry had been completed and the glue had become set, the surface was scraped and cleaned off, and well sand-papered down to make it smooth. It was then stained and polished like the walnut examples.

The quality of old marquetry varies considerably. In the floral work the "close-cutting" of the pattern is a prominent feature of the high-quality piece. To effect this perfect fit of the veneers, the cutting, both in the background and the pattern, was done on the centre of the lines of the design. In cutting the outline of the flower, the saw was kept on the outer side of the centre of the line, and in cutting the space in the background, into which it was to fit, the saw-cut would be kept on the inner side of the centre of the line. The result was that no more than a hair crack was visible between the two when they were fitted together. From examples extant of Charles II marquetry this attention to close-cutting of the inlay could not have been considered in the same degree as it was in the later pieces. On marquetry, such as the seaweed and arabesque, and in the cutting of the small packets of veneers in the floral marquetry, such close-cutting was not possible, as the veneers being all cut together there would always be between them the thickness of the saw-cut. In arabesque or seaweed marquetry the edges of the scrolls and leaves should be clean-cut and accurate in the curves, whereas on poor examples they are jagged and the curves angular.

Variation in quality in the execution of marquetry is specially noticeable when English and Dutch examples are compared. The latter is coarser and the pattern does not fit closely to the background; the design is more detached and has not the same graceful composition of the English example. Shading is more largely resorted to, and ivory inlay is also more lavishly used. The Dutch favoured the "all-over" style of marquetry, and but seldom placed their floral marquetry in panels. This is more especially true of Dutch marquetry furniture of the eighteenth century, as an early type of coarse marquetry, composed of a design of broad acanthus leaf

PLATE XXVII

Collection of Robert Frank

(Left) A bureau overlaid with walnut veneer supported on turned legs with serpentine stretcher, circa 1685.

(Right) A bureau overlaid with burr walnut veneer supported on turned and tapered legs, circa 1710.

scrolls, will sometimes be met with in panels. This type of Dutch marquetry often has birds, sometimes resembling eagles, introduced into its design, and, not unfrequently, it will be met with executed on a light background, which method the Dutch were not as averse from using as the English. Unlike the English, the Dutch continued to make floral marquetry right through the eighteenth century, its execution and design becoming more decadent as the century advanced.

In a piece of untouched marquetry, the box or holly, originally of a light colour, will have assumed a deep mellow tone, which resembles the colour often seen on the bowl of a meerschaum pipe coloured by nicotine, and is caused through the toning of the polish or varnish by long exposure to the atmosphere. The box and holly inlay will also exhibit a number of small cracks which, owing to their having become filled with dirt and wax, are specially noticeable. The surface of the marquetry, through shrinkage of the foundation on which it is laid, will be wrinkled and cracked, and portions of it, through wear and bad usage, will often be missing, disclosing the carcase. When the inlay has become loose, dirt and dust will have lodged under its surface, and where the various pieces of inlaid veneer join each other, there will be seen protruding above the surface minute ridges of hardened glue. This latter feature is typical of marquetry when in its original state, as these ridges will have been removed if the surface has been repolished. In this case the mellow tone of the box or holly will have become lighter and of a brighter yellow colour, owing to the original varnish or polish being cleaned off preparatory to the application of the new polish.

The beauty of old marquetry, to-day, as in the case of walnut furniture, depends to a great degree on the presence of patina; and a piece which has had its damaged marquetry restored, its blemishes removed, and surface coated with a high polish, can in no wise bear comparison with the piece that possesses its original surface, mellowed and patinated by time, and unharmed by the hand of the French polisher.

Spurious Marquetry Furniture

Marquetry furniture, unfortunately, is not immune from the attentions of the faker. Not only does he make examples of entirely new construction, but he enhances in value old pieces of plain walnut by the addition of spurious inlay.

The productions of the commercial faker are not of great account as, like his walnut furniture, they have but little in common with the genuine examples, either in patina, quality, or design. He generally employs sea-weed marquetry in panels which he produces in a time-saving, mechanical manner, thus rendering them easier to make than the floral or arabesque designs.

The knowledge and ability of the collector will be tested, however, by the fraudulent marquetry of the skilled faker, who utilizes the floral, seaweed, and the arabesque types, and in his work follows out the methods of the old marquetry cutters. He is not able, however, to spend too much time in the production of his pieces, and the quality of their execution suffers accordingly. By one who understands old English marquetry and is familiar with the peculiarities inherent to the methods of the workmanship, and the degree of quality and finish which could be obtained when neither time nor labour were considered, the impostures of the imitator can be recognized without difficulty.

Some of the principal points in which the modern work differs from the old can be briefly stated. The modern marquetry will lack the " close-cutting " of the old ; it will also be more stereotyped and regular in appearance, exhibiting none of the individual conceits so often found in the work of the old craftsmen. The leaves which in the old floral marquetry were cut separately from the stems will, in modern work, often be found in one with them.

Seaweed marquetry with its series of fine scrolls is a severe test of the capabilities of the modern marquetry cutter. Being the most difficult and expensive of all types of marquetry to cut, the tendency of the imitator is to simplify this design by reducing the amount of pattern, making the scrolls larger, the fronds of the seaweed broader and more regular, and eliminating the minute offshoots of the foliage. In the old work, similar to that on the table top, Plate XIV, the ends of the fronds or scrolls are slightly rounded, the delicate rounding enabling the cutter to turn his saw more easily around the points. This refinement is generally disregarded in the modern work, the fronds ending in a point around which the cutter is unable to work his saw without making a hole or dent, which becomes more prominent when filled with the stain and wax afterwards used in polishing.

Unless a prodigious amount of labour is expended, it is not possible for the modern work to exhibit the fine tracery of the old ; and the faker with a lively sense of the collector's deficient understanding of the qualities in the old marquetry does not consider it necessary to put the amount of detail into his work that would tend to avert detection. Cutting the veneers in double or quadruple thicknesses which, when opened out, form the complete panel, is one method much favoured by the imitator for reducing his labour. The " contra " or reverse veneers resulting from the cutting are also used for a second piece of furniture, which is the reason why so many of the spurious pieces exhibit marquetry with a dark pattern on a light background.

In pieces of new construction, old material will be employed for the carcase work, and genuine walnut veneer, obtained from derelict specimens, for the general surfacing. The enhancing in value of genuine pieces of plain walnut furniture by inlaying their surfaces with spurious marquetry, is a deception which the imitator has carried out on many genuine articles, such as secretaires with fall-down fronts, long-case clocks, chests-with-drawers, bureaux, and mirror frames, in fact any plain walnut piece that he considers can be increased in value successfully by this treatment. His method in this direction is to cut out pieces of the genuine walnut veneer and to fill in the vacant spaces with spurious marquetry panels. There are several advantages for the faker in this class of deception, because he is able to retain the carcase and cross-banded mouldings of the old piece and all its original veneer, except where the latter has been cut away. The modern veneer, as previously mentioned, is thinner than the old, and a thick backing of glue is required to bring the new panel flush with the surrounding veneer. As, however, the new panels are usually cleaned off and polished by the faker before the glue is set, they will afterwards sink, and in consequence will be on a slightly lower level than the original surface. Not only should the collector carefully examine the marquetry panels of a piece for this defect, but he should compare the surface of the marquetry with that of the surrounding walnut. If the marquetry panels are new, their surfaces will be comparatively free from dents and scratches, and in striking contrast to the old blemished surface of the original veneer. Occasionally some ineradicable defect, such as a deep scratch, ink-stain, pot-ring or burn on the table or chest top, will be cut through and ended in a very abrupt manner by a marquetry panel, and in such cases there can be little doubt that the piece and its marquetry panels are not contemporary.

As already mentioned, old pieces with drawers may, in the course of their existence, have been fitted with two or three sets of handles, for which the drawer fronts will have been pierced in different places. But pieces decorated with marquetry panels on the drawer fronts will sometimes be found, where the back of a drawer front will disclose one or two holes made for former handles without there being any corresponding piercings through the marquetry panels on the front ; the imitator having either forgotten to make the additional piercings or been loathe to spoil the appearance of his new marquetry.

The faker's greatest stumbling-block is the turning of the new light woods to the deep and mellow shade of the old. In order to do this he has to rely on coloured polish and dirted wax, and if this toning is too sparingly

PLATE XXVIII

(Left) A bureau overlaid with burr walnut veneer on cabriole legs ending in club feet, circa 1735. *Collection of Percival D. Griffiths*

(Right) A walnut tripod table with legs terminating in lion-paw feet, circa 1735. *Collection of Captain W. F. Dickinson*

done, the wood will be too light and new in appearance. If overdone, which is more usual, the box or holly has a clouded and painted appearance, very different from the clear brilliancy of the genuine piece. It is impossible, owing to the hardness of these light-coloured woods, to tone them except in this way; for whatever is applied does not sink in, but remains on the surface, and, consequently, obscures and hides the wood. These heavy coatings of polish and wax can be seen distinctly on the light parts of the marquetry design when it is examined in a good light. A number of these fraudulent marquetry pieces are varnished, for the skilled imitator finds that by treating them in this manner he can obtain a closer resemblance to the genuine example; the varnish giving greater clarity and a less painted effect.

Another important divergence between the genuine and spurious marquetry is the absence of the little ridges of hardened glue protruding from the joints of the inlay, as already described. Polish, dirt and darkened wax are used to fill up these joints; but this filling sinks in after a short time, leaving a distinct furrow between the veneers. When detected, this feature should, in itself, arouse suspicion.

The smooth, even surface of the fraudulent piece is in striking contrast to the blemished surface of the original one, and this will be specially evident if the hand is passed over old marquetry when in an original state. To obviate the smooth surface of his pieces the faker will blister and buckle the veneer by damping and applying a hot iron, as already mentioned. An original table top or cabinet door will generally be found split owing to shrinkage. This defect will not occur in a spurious piece if old material has been used for its carcase; but when, as sometimes happens, the imitator makes the carcase from new material, a split will occur in the veneer before many months have passed. On an original piece the crack, which will be many years old, will be filled with dirt and dust, and the once sharp edges of the veneer will be worn away. In the spurious piece the split edges of the veneer will be sharp, and the crack free from dust, and where the latter traverses the holly or box veneer, it will disclose the light colour of the new wood, very different in contrast to the artificially-toned appearance of its top surface. On a genuine piece the holly or box where split will be a dark tone through the accumulation of dirt and wax.

Chairs

English chairs were seldom decorated with marquetry, and examples treated in this manner date from the first twenty years of the eighteenth century, and are usually of the type with the hooped back and shaped splat.

PLATE XXIX

Collection of Sir John Prestige

A large walnut, double-sided, pedestal writing-table, circa 1730.

The decoration is nearly always confined to small panels on the splats and on the knees of the cabriole leg, and sometimes a small panel of marquetry is found decorating the front seat-rail. Arabesque was the variety invariably used, and a favoured custom was the inlaying of an entwined and reversed monogram on the splats of the chairs ; the delineation of a monogram in this manner being much in vogue at this period. Other chairs of this time have their splats inlaid with heraldic devices.

The hooped-back chair with cabriole legs, so often found in England decorated with floral marquetry, not only on the splat, side-rails and seat-rails, but, in some examples, even on the front legs, is not of English but Dutch origin. Compared with English chairs, showing a precise and restrained use of marquetry, these over-decorated Dutch examples are in bad taste.

The imitator makes spurious chairs decorated with small marquetry panels, as these will give him less trouble to fake than carved ornament. He has also been known to inlay new panels of marquetry into genuine walnut chairs, and would no doubt have done much more in this direction, but for the scarcity of the genuine chair. The collector should not fail to scrutinize the marquetry panels on any chair that he meets with, to make certain that they have not been added within recent years.

Tables

The oblong table with drawer, described in the previous chapter, is not an unusually rare piece to find decorated with marquetry. A number of examples have survived with floral marquetry of the early type and spiral-twist legs. The later type on scroll legs with floral or seaweed marquetry is much rarer and far more valuable, to-day, than any other variety of this table.

The present condition of these marquetry tables is similar to that of the contemporary examples in oyster-shell parquetry or walnut as described on page 76. The marquetry example, however, differs in one respect in that the top of the table will often have pieces of the inlay entirely missing. Many such tables, once in this condition, have been restored, but owing to the difficulty of matching the new parts with the old, the old will be made to match the new by repolishing the whole top. This naturally involves the destruction of the patina. The imitator has found the reproduction of this table, decorated with marquetry, a very remunerative business, and he has accordingly made many fraudulent examples from old material, using old walnut veneer for the background of the marquetry. Many of these spurious tables are decorated with seaweed marquetry in panels and

PLATE XXX

Collection of Sir John Prestige

A bookcase veneered with walnut, circa 1725.

have the rare scroll leg, as this leg not only makes the table more saleable, but it is easier to reproduce owing to its surface being veneered. For the veneering of these legs the skilled faker will use old veneer, but the backs of the legs, as in the genuine examples, he will leave unveneered. The freshly cut deal or pine exposed on this part has, therefore, to be faked, and the collector should make a point of carefully examining these unveneered portions for any signs of staining or colouring. Such parts on the genuine leg will have the dry look of the mature wood, and be smooth and not sticky to the touch. The rarity of the genuine marquetry table with the scroll leg, and the incommensurable number of fraudulent examples of this type, should, alone, make the collector pause before buying a table of this description without very careful examination on the lines already indicated.

Another difference between the fraudulent table and the old is that the tops of nine out of every ten genuine tables will have one or more cracks lengthways across the surface, caused through the marquetry splitting by the shrinkage of the carcase. As already mentioned, such defects are not likely to be found on the spurious example, and the notes on page 98, in connection with these cracks when they do occur, should also be remembered by the collector when he examines a table of this description.

Besides the spurious examples of this table, the collector must also be wary of purchasing a contemporary Dutch table at the price of an English one, as the former are not so valuable. The Dutch tables are heavier in design and of larger dimensions, their legs and stretchers being thicker and not so refined in feeling. The tops also are thicker, and their edges, instead of being cross-banded with walnut, are decorated with alternating inlaid pieces of dark and light wood, or sometimes of ivory and ebony.

Other types of tables decorated with marquetry are but seldom met with to-day, and unless specially favoured by fortune, the oblong table is the only genuine English marquetry table the collector is likely to meet with. It must not be inferred, however, from this scarcity that other types of marquetry tables were not made, but rather that they were not so fashionable or popular as the oblong variety. An example of a rare type of table to be found in marquetry is shown in Plate XIV.

The discovery of a genuine marquetry card table does not appear to have been recorded. The commercial imitator has, however, supplied the demands of the unconversant collector by the production of scores of such tables decorated, usually, with seaweed marquetry in panels. The cloudy and muddy appearance of these pieces with their artificial painted patina does not require much perspicuity to detect, even were the collector unaware that the existence of genuine examples of such card tables is doubtful.

PLATE XXXI

Collection of J. Thursby Pelham

(Top) A walnut circular-top card table, supported on turned and tapered legs connected by stretchers, circa 1700.

Collection of Percival D. Griffiths

(Bottom) A walnut card table with the knees of cabriole legs decorated with eagles' heads, circa 1725.

Cabinets

As already mentioned, the cabinet-with-doors mounted on a stand or base with drawers, dating from the first half of the walnut period, is often met with in marquetry, and the note given in the last chapter on the design and rarity of the stands applies also to marquetry examples.

The small drawers in the interiors of these cabinets will have their fronts decorated with marquetry; and the insides of the doors and the sides of the cabinets will also be treated with this decoration. The colour of the wood on the fronts of the interior drawers and the inside of the doors will in many cabinets be found to vary from that on the exterior; the light-coloured woods on the outside will have the deep mellow tone already described, whereas inside the cabinet they will usually be much lighter and fresher in appearance. This is due to the varnish or polish, not being exposed to the atmosphere, remaining unchanged.

Larger examples of these cabinets, similar to the one illustrated, Plate X, are more usually met with in marquetry, and not in oyster-shell parquetry. The early examples of this cabinet, both large and small, were decorated with floral marquetry, the doors being divided up into small panels, and the reserves between the panels filled with oyster-shell parquetry either of laburnum or olive wood, and occasionally with straight-cut walnut veneer. In these floral marquetry examples it will be noticed that the panels of marquetry, even on the small drawers in the interior of the cabinet, are all of different design. The fact that the designs were never repeated shows what painstaking care was devoted to making the best furniture of this period. These cabinets are seldom found to-day decorated with seaweed marquetry, and like the tables, very few are extant on stands with the rare scroll legs.

A few other cabinets of unusual design decorated with marquetry have survived, but in such small numbers that they cannot be regarded as standard types of which many examples were made, like the cabinets already described. One of these rare pieces, the cabinet or wardrobe reputed to have been made for James II when Duke of York, is shown in Plate XI. The marquetry is of exceptionally high quality, and the piece lavishly inlaid without regard to cost. Both in design and execution this cabinet is English in character,* yet, as its date is about 1680, it is unlikely, in the short time marquetry had been in vogue at this date, that an English craftsman could have become sufficiently skilled in the art of marquetry cutting as to produce such an elaborate and finished piece. It was probably, therefore, the work of Dutch

* As a further proof of the English provenience of this piece the locks, which are the original ones, are English.

craftsmen, resident in this country. At the same time the support of the massive cabinet on arcading, resting on the four ball feet in front, is ungainly, and the effect is not good in proportion. It would suggest that the designer's original intention was to mount the cabinet on a stand, but finding the piece would be too heavy, altered his design, as the construction shows no evidence of there having been any legs, and the ball feet are contemporary.

So far as the imitator is concerned, these marquetry cabinets will not be found of entirely new construction, for they involve so much labour in their production that it would not pay to make them. As already mentioned, very few were made in the straight-cut walnut, so that examples enhanced in value by the addition of spurious marquetry panels are less likely to be met with.

Of china cabinets or bookcases with glazed fronts decorated with marquetry, no genuine English examples are known to exist; although the commercial faker, whose walnut china cabinets have already been commented upon, often varies their design by making specimens inlaid with marquetry panels. The Dutch walnut china cabinets, as already described on page 82, will be met with in marquetry, and these should not be mistaken for English examples. The marquetry which decorates these eighteenth-century cabinets is generally of floral design, coarsely and poorly executed, and is not in panels but covers the whole of the cupboard doors or drawer-fronts. The light woods of this Dutch marquetry are usually of a bright yellow colour and garish in appearance.

Secretaires and Writing-Bureaux

The secretaire with the fall-down front, introduced into England about 1675, and described in the last chapter, is the only piece of furniture decorated with marquetry made for writing purposes, of which a number of examples have survived, although these marquetry secretaires are outnumbered by the examples of the marquetry cabinet with solid doors just described. These secretaires are found decorated in panels both with the early floral marquetry and also with the later seaweed variety.

As already mentioned, a number of spurious examples of the secretaire have been made in recent years by enhancing the genuine plain walnut ones with marquetry panels. Such examples the collector should be careful to avoid purchasing.

Examples of the early bureaux-on-legs, decorated with seaweed and arabesque marquetry, have also survived, but rare as are the plain walnut examples of this bureau, the marquetry examples are still rarer. To enrich his copies of the early bureau-on-legs, the imitator will sometimes decorate them with panels of seaweed marquetry.

Of the bureau-on-drawers, and the bureau-bookcase, only a few specimens in marquetry are extant, and these are decorated with panels of the seaweed variety. No example of either of these articles decorated with floral designs is recorded, for the reason that these pieces were only introduced into England when the floral marquetry was on the wane. Many Dutch bureaux-on-drawers will, however, be met with, decorated with the characteristic coarse marquetry of floral design. These examples date from the middle of the eighteenth century or later, for the Dutch, as already noted, continued to make marquetry furniture long after it had gone out of fashion in England. The Dutch bureaux are usually of much larger dimensions than the English, and the lower part occasionally has the *bombé*, or swelled front, that is so typical of the eighteenth-century Dutch furniture.

A number of genuine walnut bureaux and bureau-bookcases have been converted into marquetry examples within recent years, and this fact should be remembered by the collector when he meets with either of these pieces decorated with inlay.

The small bureau-on-stand decorated with marquetry would be a very rare find to-day, for although such pieces must doubtless have been made, the existence of one does not appear to be known. Many of the fraudulent examples of the imitator, are, however, decorated with seaweed marquetry.

The secretaire with knee-hole and let-down front would also be a very rare piece if found in marquetry. Plain examples, which have been enhanced with spurious marquetry panels, are more likely to be met with to-day than the genuine specimen.

Chests-with-Drawers and Chests-on-Stands

Chests-with-drawers, like the other marquetry furniture, were decorated with floral marquetry in panels, floral marquetry of the "all-over" type, seaweed marquetry in panels, and late examples in the arabesque marquetry, according to the varying fashions between 1670 and 1700. The marquetry chest-on-stand does not appear to have been made after 1690, and, therefore, examples with seaweed or arabesque marquetry are not likely to be met with. This is borne out by the fact that the taller chest-on-stand of the William and Mary period, without the veneered top, is never found decorated with inlay.

Chests-with-drawers have survived in far larger numbers than those on stands, and the notes already given on the stands of the walnut examples, both as regards their design and rarity, also refer equally well to marquetry specimens.

PLATE XXXII

Collection of Percival D. Griffiths

A walnut card table with lion masks decorating knees of legs. Front of table serpentine in shape, circa 1735.

The tops of these chests are inlaid with marquetry similar in the design to that on the tops of the oblong tables already described. In fact, this similarity has often induced the imitator to convert a chest top into a table top. As a table is more valuable to-day than a chest, it would pay him to carry out this fraud, even though he has to make a new drawer and frame, legs and stretchers.

Besides this conversion, the marquetry chest-with-drawers is a piece that has often assisted the imitator to reap a good profit. Scores of plain walnut chests during the last twenty years have had marquetry panels let into their surfaces, and although this deceit in the past was a very paying proposition, when the plain example could be purchased for £3 or £4, to-day it is not so frequently carried out, as the plain chest is not only much scarcer, but considerably more expensive.

A type of marquetry that was much favoured by the imitator for decorating these chests was the Dutch design of the broad acanthus-leaf scroll already mentioned. This marquetry being coarser, and having no fine detail in its pattern, could be reproduced more easily and at a lower cost than the floral, seaweed or arabesque varieties. Chests decorated with this foreign type of coarse marquetry should therefore receive but scant attention from the collector. A useful test to apply to these chests to determine their genuineness, is the one already mentioned of the holes at the back of the drawer-fronts not appearing on the face of the front because they have been covered up with the modern marquetry.

Clock-Cases

The long-case clock made its first appearance in England soon after Charles II ascended the throne. The case was a favourite article to be decorated with marquetry; so much so, that the evolution of English marquetry can be traced in the clock-cases from 1670–1720.

The earliest clock-cases, dating from about 1662, were veneered with ebony (Plate XV (*a* and *c*)). The next type of case would appear, from examples extant, to have been decorated with oyster-shell parquetry, and sometimes further enhanced with inlaid stars on the door and base (Plate XV (*b*)). This was followed by the case with floral marquetry in panels (Plate XVI (*a*)). By about 1690 clock-cases with marquetry of floral design entirely covering the door and base came into vogue, and some examples are found of this type with cupids and scroll work introduced into the design which, as already described, was due at this time to Daniel Marot and his followers. Cases decorated with seaweed marquetry date from about 1695, and the design is generally in panels. The clock-case with arabesque is, to-day, usually associated with cases dating from 1705–1720 (Plate XVI (*b*)). The dates given here are, of course, only approximate, as the various styles in marquetry overlapped, floral marquetry cases being found of as late a date as 1715.

The craft of the clockmaker in the time of Charles II was an important one. The celebrated horologists, such as John Fromanteel and Thomas Tompion, held rank in their day as scientists, and enjoyed the esteem of contemporary society. Through the inventions and improvements made during this reign, foremost amongst which were the long pendulum and anchor escapement, the popularity of the clock quickly became assured. The earlier timekeeper, the brass lantern clock with the bob pendulum, had been but an indifferent instrument to tell the passing of the hours.

The long-case clock when first introduced was, as one would expect, confined to the patronage of the rich; but the demand for it continually increasing caused considerable numbers to be made, more especially from the reign of William and Mary onwards, which can be with reason inferred from the long roll of members of the Clockmakers' Company at that time.

The early clocks were narrow and small in size, with dials about 10 inches square, or even smaller. The sizes of the dials and the cases increased as time went on, and the moulding under the hood, also that surmounting the base, altered in section, the earlier ones being invariably convex and the later ones concave; this change coming into vogue about 1705. In the earlier cases up to about 1695, the hoods slid up to give access to the dial for the winding of the movement, but after that date the hood was provided with a door.

Other changes that took place were variations in the ornaments which decorated the four spandrel corners of the dial; the figures which indicated the minutes on the dial also gradually increased in size, as the early clocks had the figures small. An important change which came in about 1715 to 1720 was the addition of an arched top to the previous square dial.

The cases in this period were made, unquestionably, by cabinet-makers who confined their work solely to the production of such articles. This would account for clock-cases having certain peculiarities not found in contemporary furniture. For instance, the mouldings around the doors in some cases are made in the solid wood, ebonized in the Dutch manner, and not cross-banded. On other cases decorated with marquetry, the panels would appear to have been cut away to make them fit the door or base. Such examples were undoubtedly made by small country clock-case makers, who bought stock marquetry panels, and did not cut their own marquetry as the case-makers in the larger towns would undoubtedly have done. The carcases of the cases at this period were invariably made of oak for the sake of appearance, owing to the interior of the case being visible when the door was open.

The movements of the long-case clocks of this period are a factor in their present-day value, apart from the cases ; in fact, to-day a fine movement governs the value of a clock even more than the case. A case which possesses a movement by one of the famous makers of this period, such as John Fromanteel, William Clement, Thomas Tompion (clock and watch-maker to Charles II), Edward East, Daniel Quare, Joseph Knibb, or George Graham, will be of great interest and value to the clock collector.

Movements by these makers, needless to say, are extremely rare and much sought after to-day ; although clocks with movements by contemporary and less eminent makers are not so difficult to meet with, and such examples will have their value governed to a greater extent by their cases.

A few interesting points about clock movements may be briefly stated here. Movements exhibit varying degrees of quality ; those made by London makers being markedly superior to the movements made by the country maker. Fine specimens by the best makers show a high standard of workmanship in the finish, not only of the dials and hands, but of the corner-pieces, which on the earliest examples are water-gilt ; also of the hand-beaten brass plates, the pillars which hold them together, and the wheels and pinions. In poor quality movements the plates will be thick and the wheels and pinions coarser and more roughly cut. In the best examples the pillars will be held in position by hooks which fit into a groove in the part of the pillar that protrudes through the plate ; but in specimens of poorer quality the ends of the pillars will be drilled through, and a tapered pin wedged through the hole.

The majority of the clocks of this period have eight-day movements ; rarer and more valuable examples will require winding once a month ; while some exceptional and rare movements will go for six or twelve months. One of the features of a high quality movement was the provision for maintaining power, so that the clock continued to go during the operation of winding. The mechanism for maintaining power was brought into action by pulling a cord, and in order that this should not be forgotten before winding, two little shutters closed the holes in the dial, covering the winding squares ; these shutters being drawn back from the apertures by the same cord that brought the maintaining power into operation. Many clocks will have lost their shutters and maintaining power, but a movement originally made with this feature can generally be recognized because the ends of the winding squares do not protrude through the holes in the dial, but will be slightly recessed to allow the shutters, which are at the back of the dial, to slide in front of them. Clocks without the winding holes in the dial are

PLATE XXXIII

Collection of Mrs. T. D. Wilson

A chest-with-drawers on stand overlaid with walnut veneer. Height, 5 feet, 9 inches, circa 1705.

30-hour movements, wound up by pulling the cords or chains of the weights. These are not found dating from the walnut period and are of no interest to the collector. Oak clock-cases also do not belong to this period, oak being used for the cheaper provincial clock-cases made in the last half of the eighteenth century, at which time the clock came into the homes of the lower classes.

The weights on a clock of good quality will be encased in brass, whereas, on inferior movements they will be of lead or iron and uncased. The arrangement by which the door of the hood is secured with a bolt, which can only be released by opening the long door, is to ensure that the long door is opened before the winding is started. The person winding will then be able to see the weights, and note when they reach the top of the case, showing that the clock is fully wound. Otherwise, if the weights are not visible, there is a danger of over-winding and of the weights striking the clock-board and straining or breaking the gut.

Many clock movements are spurious, the names of famous makers they bear having been engraved on the dials in recent years. A large number of high quality movements of this period have been ruined by the works being renovated and altered. If the back-plate of a clock shows a number of empty holes which originally held pinions, it denotes that some part of the original movement is missing, and this, to a certain degree, depreciates the value. In some cases, close examination will show that an attempt has been made to disguise the absence of original parts by stopping up these holes.

This period of clocks with ebony, parquetry, marquetry and walnut cases is the most interesting to the clock collector, as it includes the productions of the most famous English clockmakers, and the movements are, accordingly, of exceptional interest.

From the end of the walnut period to that of the eighteenth century, clock movements declined in quality, especially in the execution and finish of the dials and hands. No fine month or year movements belong to this period, as the clock had now become a standard article of domestic furniture to be found in every home. By the close of the eighteenth century clock movements of high quality were again made, this period being specially of interest for its regulators ; and a number of domestic clocks, dating from the early nineteenth century, exhibit the fine finish and quality of the regulator type. The clocks of this revival have naturally engaged the collector's attention, although in a lesser degree than the clocks of the walnut period.

The cases of the long-case clocks have not been overlooked by the imitator, as he has inlaid many plain walnut examples with spurious panels

PLATE XXXIV

(Left) A knee-hole pedestal dressing-table overlaid with walnut veneer, circa 1735. *Collection of Patrick Hastings, K. C.*

(Right) A dressing-table on cabriole legs terminating in claw and ball feet, circa 1730. *Collection of Percival D. Griffiths*

of marquetry. Although a number of genuine seaweed and arabesque marquetry cases will be met with in which the inlay is a dark pattern on a light background, many more spurious examples of this description will be found to-day, owing to the imitator using the " contra " veneers left over from the cutting, which he employs to decorate a second clock-case. These spurious cases invariably have the pattern symmetrical, because, as already mentioned, this device considerably lessens the labour in cutting and designing the marquetry.

The rare type of arabesque marquetry, known as the " Persian," will also be met with on spurious cases, in fact many more spurious examples of this type exist than genuine ones. Sometimes the imitator, in order to give his marquetry clocks a more genuine appearance, will coat their surfaces very heavily with thick, opaque varnish to reproduce the condition in which the genuine clocks are occasionally found.

In regard to the commercial imitator, his efforts on long-case clocks would appear to be confined to examples of the small long-case clock, known to-day as the " Grandmother " clock. Genuine long-case clocks of this small size, especially of the walnut period, are very few and far between ; in fact, it would not be an exaggeration to say that it is doubtful whether half-a-dozen are in existence. The spurious grandmother clocks generally have modern movements,* faked to give them an appearance of age, and the cases will be found in walnut, burr walnut, marquetry, lacquer and mahogany.

A number of genuine clocks which in the past had either their bases or the domes of their hoods removed to reduce their height and permit them to stand in low rooms, will be found, to-day, with the bases or the domes restored. The collector should, therefore, carefully examine these parts for restoration, and notice any variation in the cutting of the marquetry and also in its surface condition. Sometimes clocks will be found with half the base restored only, whereas in others the whole base will be modern. Many of these will have a crack across the marquetry panel, and the collector should remember the remarks already given on the light colour of the box-wood on its split edges.

Many old cases, both in walnut and marquetry, had their patina destroyed by modern polishing, whilst others, as already noted, will be found heavily coated with a thick, opaque varnish. Fortunately, the latter, if carefully removed, does not damage the appearance of the clock to the same extent as those that have had their surfaces scraped and polished. It should be

* Sometimes old movements obtained from the hood or wall clocks, which have small dials, are used. Genuine examples of these clocks, contemporary with the walnut clocks, are to be found, having thirty-hour movements of poor quality. They are, however, of little value to-day.

noted that genuine examples which have been repolished will not show the furrows between the inlay to the same degree as in the modern marquetry.

Bracket Clocks

Bracket clocks of the Charles II period, unlike the long-case movements, had the bob pendulum with the crown wheel escapement, similar to the earlier lantern clocks ; but the driving power instead of being derived from weights, was obtained from a spring enclosed in a brass barrel. The improved anchor escapement was not adapted to the bracket clock until late in the eighteenth century, although a large number of movements have had the crown-wheel escapement altered at a subsequent date because of its irregularity. The back-plates of the bracket clocks, unlike those of the long-case clocks, are invariably engraved ; examples of the first half of the walnut period have square dials with cases veneered with ebony or with pear-wood ebonized. They are termed " Basket Top " clocks, being surmounted by a bell-shaped dome which is composed sometimes of wood with brass mounts, whilst others will have the basket top made entirely of brass of pierced design. In some fine and very rare examples the basket-top, mounts and dial will be of silver instead of brass. A few very rare basket-top clocks of this type have survived with tortoise-shell cases or veneered walnut cases, and such examples are much sought after by the collector.

In the eighteenth century, the bracket clock, like the long-case clock, had an arched dial (see Plate XL (*a* and *b*)), and the clock was higher and not so square in shape. Examples of this type usually have pear-wood ebonized cases ; and, although in lesser number, specimens with lacquer cases have also survived. The quality of the movements of the early bracket clocks is exceptionally fine. Specimens with chiming movements will also be found, but it should be noted that this feature does not enhance their value as it would do if found on the movement of a long-case clock.

The imitator does not pay so much attention to the bracket clock as he does to the long-case variety, although he has been known to re-veneer with old walnut veneer the early ebonized case, and, in some instances, has also made marquetry specimens. The transformation of an ebonized bracket clock into a tortoise-shell example is also not a very difficult conversion ; but the imitator is unlikely to copy the genuine English example by making the mouldings of the case in tortoise-shell, as this would incur too much expense, and he therefore retains the ebonized mouldings. Many of the later bracket clocks with the arched dial have been converted into lacquer specimens, but these will be dealt with in the chapter on that subject.

Mirrors

The only mirrors which have survived in any number from the first half of the walnut period have heavy moulded frames with hoods, and are of a similar design to the marquetry example, Plate XIII. These mirrors will be found with the straight-cut walnut veneer, with oyster-shell parquetry, and in marquetry; of the last named the earlier specimens have their frames inlaid with floral marquetry in panels, whilst in others the marquetry design covers the whole frame, similar to the one illustrated. Mirrors of this type are also extant, dating from the reign of William III, decorated with seaweed marquetry in panels.

This mirror is found in various sizes, but it was invariably designed with a hood with a shaped top, which, in some cases, was ornamented with a pierced design, whilst in others it was plain. The hoods were fixed with two wooden tongues, which fitted into slots in the back of the frame, but owing to the fragile nature of the hood, the majority of the mirrors will be found with this feature missing. A mirror without its hood is an imperfect specimen, and its value is depreciated in consequence. In proof that the hood is missing, examination of the back of the frame will show the slots into which the tongues originally fitted.

Another loss which many of these mirrors have sustained is that of the original Vauxhall mirror-plate. This, also, has a detrimental effect to the mirror's present-day value, as the old plate with shallow bevelling and dark reflection is in perfect harmony with its walnut frame, whereas the new one, with its clear reflection and sharp bevelling, is out of character.

Owing to the fact that many more mirrors of this description have survived with plain walnut frames, many such examples have had their value fictitiously enhanced within recent years by spurious inlay.

Other types of mirrors decorated with marquetry are much scarcer to-day, which is perhaps due to the walnut-frame mirror declining in favour in the William and Mary period, when mirrors with gilt, lacquer and glass frames, came into vogue. The mirror with gilt frame must have been particularly popular from 1700 onwards, as a large number of examples dating from the second half of the walnut period are in existence to-day.

Lace Boxes and other Articles Decorated with Marquetry

An article of which a large number must have been made, as many have survived, is the shallow box with lid, which is known to-day as a lace box. Examples extant are generally decorated either with floral marquetry in panels, or with oyster-shell parquetry.

PLATE XXXV

(Left) A walnut cheval fire-screen with octagonal panel of petit point needlework with gros point border, circa 1725. *Collection of Frank Partridge*

(Right) A walnut tripod pole fire-screen with panel of petit point needlework, circa 1730. *Collection of Percival D. Griffiths*

A number of draught or chess boards, made in the shape of shallow boxes, which, when folded out flat, form the playing board, are extant decorated with inlay. These are of great rarity, and of considerable value and interest, especially if the draughts or chessmen have also been preserved. Among other articles treated with marquetry were bellows, but these are only known by two or three existing examples.

Owing to the vogue for marquetry in the late seventeenth century, it must have been used for decorating a number of other articles of domestic furniture which have not, unfortunately, survived in sufficient numbers to warrant their special notice. For instance, the dressing-table with drawers, supported on legs of the type similar to Plate XXXIV (*b*), is not unknown in marquetry, and there is still a likelihood that among the hidden treasures in England other rare specimens of marquetry furniture will one day come to light.

CHAPTER VI

QUEEN ANNE AND GEORGIAN WALNUT FURNITURE

1702–1745

THE furniture of the latter half of the walnut period, as we know it to-day, is plain in character, with little enrichment by carving or inlay; relying for its decorative effect on good proportion, graceful and elegant form, and on the figure and marking of the wood; exhibiting also, workmanship of the highest quality. Refined and tasteful, it is perhaps of all types of English furniture the most characteristic; possessing an individuality and artistic beauty that ensures for it a prominent place in the annals of English furniture.

The desire for luxury and domestic comfort disclosed in the first half of the walnut period had extended to the upper and middle classes, and was no longer confined to the wealthy. To meet the greater demand for walnut furniture, the use of which now became general, it was made on more standardized lines in considerably larger quantities; and this explains why most of the veneered walnut furniture existing to-day, dates from the latter half of the walnut period. New types of furniture were introduced; and the evolution of previous types brought about alterations in design according to the changing fashions.

Burr walnut succeeded oyster-shell parquetry, and the use of marquetry was now confined to small panels of a restrained design in seaweed or arabesque; this, however, does not refer to the clock-cases, the production of which, as already noted, was a craft separate from that of the furniture maker. Carving was confined to decoration on the legs of chairs, stools, settees, and other leg furniture; also to the decoration of the backs of chairs and settees, for which the carving was executed in a very low relief and applied, as already described, on the surface of the veneer. This limitation of decoration by carving and inlay was compensated for by the fine figure and markings of the wood; and the skilful arrangement of these natural features is the distinguishing characteristic of the veneered furniture. The use of well-defined mouldings, all of which were made from cross-cut walnut, also contributed to the decorative effect.

In the previous period all leg furniture, such as chairs, stools, and couches, and the stands of chests and cabinets, had the legs connected by stretchers. One of the important changes that now occurred in furniture design lay in the discarding of these stretchers, an alteration undoubtedly evoked by the development of the cabriole leg, the designers being rightly convinced that the stretcher marred the contour of the leg.

During the reign of Queen Anne the cabriole leg was light in design and followed the form and outline of the William and Mary examples. The *pied de biche* and the scroll foot, the usual terminations for the earliest examples of this leg, were superseded by the square-moulded foot (see Plate XVII (*a*)); the club foot (see Plate XVIII (*a*)); and the spade foot, (see Plate XVII (*d*)). Other variants were made, notably the square-club foot, with which the leg was also square (Plate XXXIII). The legs with these terminations had but little decoration in the way of carving on the knee. Those with the spade foot and the club foot were sometimes decorated with an ornament in the form of husks, but more often with the escallop shell (see Plate XXI). Both *motifs*, combined together sometimes, were much in vogue during the first thirty years of the eighteenth century; and the shell was not only extensively used for decorating the knees of cabriole legs, but figures as an ornament on the backs of chairs and settees, on the gilt mirror frames of the period, and also found its way into the design of arabesque marquetry.

By the end of Queen Anne's reign, the cabriole leg, now freed from the stretcher, had a bolder contour, and became heavier and more important; and with this bolder type of leg the well-known claw-and-ball foot appeared. The now greater breadth of the knee called for more elaborate treatment than it had hitherto received; and although the shell, in a more ornate form, was extensively used with the claw-and-ball foot, a number of other *motifs* for decorating the knee were laid under contribution. Acanthus foliage (see Plate XXII), was one very frequently used, but a more decorative *motif* was the lion mask* (see Plate XXXII), which made its appearance about 1725.

This feature on the knee originated another terminal for the leg, which, when decorated with this mask, invariably ended in a lion's-paw foot.† The paw-foot was, however, more often employed without the accompaniment of the mask; and with the claw-and-ball foot, and the earlier

* The origin of the lion mask on the knee of the cabriole leg is difficult to surmise. It was most probably an alternative *motif* to the satyr mask, which is found decorating the knees of the cabriole legs of gilt furniture at this period, and was adapted from the contemporary Louis Quatorze furniture. The satyr mask or "Indian's Head," as it is sometimes called, is not unknown on mahogany furniture, a few exceptional pieces having this rare *motif*.

† There are two varieties of the paw-foot; one similar to that on the card-table, Plate XXXII, and the other of a plainer design, similar to the feet of the settee, Plate XXII.

PLATE XXXVI

Collection of C. H. F. Kinderman

(Top) A knee-hole secretaire overlaid with burr walnut veneer, circa 1700. (The original bracket feet of this piece are missing.)

Collection of Geoffrey D. Hobson

(Bottom) A knee-hole pedestal dressing table, of Oriental workmanship, decorated with black and gold lacquer, circa 1725. (The handles of this piece are not original.)

club-foot, made the three principal terminals for the cabriole leg from 1725 up to the end of the period ; the club-foot being used for the plain and inexpensive furniture. Another " animal " *motif* introduced about 1715, and therefore prior to the lion mask, was that of the eagle head,* and this was, also, occasionally employed on the knees of cabriole legs (see Plate XXXI (*b*)). Both the eagle and the lion head were used for the terminations of the arms of chairs and settees ; and the eagle head, like the shell, was often employed for the decoration of gilt mirror frames.

The elaboration of carved ornament appearing in the furniture of about 1720–5 may have been due to the introduction of mahogany, as the cabinet-makers, realizing what a good medium this wood was for carving, no doubt felt the necessity for further enriching their furniture so that this quality in the new, fashionable wood might be utilized to advantage. This assumption is supported by the fact that the majority of the chairs, settees and stools, on which carved decoration was employed to any extent, are in mahogany and not in walnut. As on the introduction of walnut, chairs were the first articles to be made of it, so they were the first for which walnut was superseded by mahogany ; and although walnut chairs were made as late as 1750 in the French taste which was then prevailing, there are many more chairs, dating from 1720 to the end of the period, in mahogany than there are in walnut. Some mahogany examples are, perhaps, before 1720, which would be early for this wood.

As already mentioned on page 22, plain veneered walnut furniture, such as bureaux, bureau-bookcases, tallboys, chests-with-drawers, long-case clocks and dressing-tables, unlike the chairs, continued to be made up to the end of the walnut period ; and where there is a paucity of articles made in walnut, they will be found in mahogany, the converse also holding good. When mahogany furniture came into vogue about 1725-30, all the best qualty furniture after this date was made from this wood, leaving the plainer furniture for the less wealthy classes to be made from walnut. Superlative pieces of walnut dating from 1725 to the end of the period are, therefore, exceptional, and, consequently, extremely rare.

Gilding, as already noted in Chapter I, was used in a very restrained manner as a means of enriching walnut furniture; but it was confined to the best class of furniture in this period. The carved decoration and the mouldings of a piece were the parts treated with the gilding.

* The eagle-head *motif*, similar to the lion mask, also affected the design of the foot of the cabriole leg, as on some examples where the knee is decorated with this bird *motif*, the claws and the leg will be decorated with scaling in imitation of that of a bird (see Plate XXXI).

Chairs, Stools, Settees, and Couches

The chair, of all leg furniture, was the last to lose its stretchers, as on tables and stands they were discarded in the early years of the century; but turned stretchers are found on chairs as late as 1720, although by 1710 the majority were made without them.

The high, carved hooped back of the William and Mary chair became lower in the first decade of the eighteenth century, and the splat, side-rails and seat-rails were overlaid with walnut veneer. With the advent of the bolder cabriole leg the front corners of the seat, which, previously, had been angular, now became rounded (see Plate XIX (*a*)), and chairs with this seat would appear to have been made up to about 1730.

The wooden chair-back settee was an innovation, for in the previous period, as already noted, the couches were not made with wooden backs. These settees were designed with two and three chair-backs; the two-chair-back variety having three legs, and that with the three-chair-backs having four legs in front, these front legs lining with the uprights to the back, as can be seen in the examples illustrated, Plates XXI, XXII, and XXIII (*a*).

The upholstered-back couch of the first half of the walnut period continued to be made in the latter half, the legs following the designs of the chairs, but examples of a later date than 1725 appear to have been confined to mahogany. A variant of this upholstered-back couch was one with dimensions of a very large arm-chair; and, unlike the ordinary size couches, it had two legs in front instead of three, and the back was lower. This type of small couch has been termed a "love seat."

Besides the upholstered-back couch, chairs, both single and arm, were made with upholstered backs; and an example is illustrated in Plate XX (*a*) of an arm-chair, which, owing to its late date, is but rarely found in walnut, most examples of this type being in mahogany. This specimen is covered with needlework, which became very fashionable during the first half of the eighteenth century, entire suites of furniture being upholstered with it, as may be gathered from the particulars of the suite sold at the Wanstead House sale, mentioned on page 18. This needlework was usually of floral design, sometimes of flowers in vases, and, occasionally, with centre panels of figures in landscapes surrounded by floral borders. It varied in quality according to the fineness of the stitch, the coarser stitch being known to-day as *gros point*, and the finer as *petit point*; some of this needlework shows the two stitches in combination, the flowers being in the fine, and the background in the coarse stitch, whilst a large quantity will be found in the coarse stitch only.

These chairs, stools and settees, both with the wooden and the upholstered backs, were originally made in suites, consisting of six or a dozen single chairs, two or more arm-chairs, with, perhaps, two or four stools, and two settees. The walnut suite sold at Wanstead House, already referred to, consisted of ten chairs and two settees.

The winged arm-chair of this half of the period would appear to have been seldom made in walnut after the introduction of the claw-and-ball foot, as all existing examples with this foot or the paw-foot are usually of mahogany. The earlier type of winged arm-chair with the small cabriole plain legs, sometimes connected by stretchers and ending in the spade-foot, or, as in example illustrated, Plate XVIII (*b*), in the club-foot, was the type generally made in walnut.

Another type of chair in walnut is a small arm-chair, sometimes with upholstered back (see Plate XX (*b*)), and sometimes with a shaped, solid, veneered back. Such chairs were used for writing, and are known to-day as writing-chairs. Another variety of writing-chair is the corner chair, but this being a type introduced about 1725, few examples are met with in walnut. A variation of this corner chair had a shaped, and generally, solid splat fitted on to the back, similar to Plate XVIII (*a*). Chairs of this description, called barber's chairs, were used for the purpose of shaving, the high splat forming a support for the head. The best examples of these two types of chairs have all four legs cabriole, similar to the example illustrated, but the more usual variety has only one cabriole leg in front, the remaining three being straight and ending in club-feet.

Present-Day Condition of Chairs, Stools, Settees, and Couches

These articles will rarely be met with in sets as originally made. A set of six chairs is of considerable value, to-day, especially if the legs terminate in the claw-and-ball feet, and the knees are decorated with carving. As already mentioned, the collector is much more likely to find such a set in mahogany.

The single chairs, like those of the early period, are usually found either as single specimens or in pairs; the arm-chairs are less likely to be met with, and then only singly. The settees are rarer than the arm-chairs, and of considerable value to-day. The three-chair-back example is a still more difficult piece to find; in fact, judging from its scarcity to-day, it could have been but seldom made. Of the upholstered-back couch, a number must have been made in the first twenty-five years of the century, but few have survived, and these, as already stated, have the small plain cabriole leg, sometimes connected by stretchers.

PLATE XXXVII

Collection of Frank Partridge

A cabinet decorated with English red and gold lacquer on carved, wood and silvered stand, circa 1685.

The chairs, stools, and settees with the claw-and-ball terminal to the cabriole leg and the carved knee, are naturally of greater value and interest to-day than the plainer type with the club-foot. Examples with the paw-foot are still rarer and more highly esteemed, while those with carved masks or eagles' heads decorating the knees of the cabriole legs are of great rarity and value, and only a few walnut stools, chairs, and settees with these *motifs* are known to exist. The presence of a lion or eagle head on the ends of the arms of a settee or chair, although not such a rare feature, especially the eagle head, as a mask on the leg, is another factor that adds considerably to the value of an example. The furniture which is decorated with such bird or beast *motifs* represents the best and most costly furniture of its time, as such features are hardly ever to be found on pieces of poor quality. The fact that so few examples have survived in walnut, and that the majority are in mahogany, again proves how the cabinet-makers favoured the latter wood for their best furniture, and only used walnut for such pieces occasionally. In comparison, the walnut specimens are markedly superior as regards decorative value, especially when they have the wooden splat-back ; the golden colour and marking of the walnut having a far richer effect than the dark, plain Spanish mahogany used at that time.

The higher-quality chairs and settees have the splats of the back and the rails veneered with burr walnut, whereas, lower-quality examples will be overlaid with the straight-cut veneer. Unfortunately, a number of these chairs and settees have suffered from modern polishing, and these, with other walnut furniture similarly treated, are thereby depreciated in value.

Examples with the original needlework coverings are seldom to be found, although a number of chairs, settees, and stools have had their seats covered in contemporary needlework which has been restored and made to fit the articles within recent years. The presence of such old needlework, if not too much restored, on a chair, stool, or settee, adds considerably to its value ; but the collector should be wary of the chair or couch covered with a piece of old needlework which has been extended so that it covers the back, seat and arms, whereas, before this increase in size, it was hardly large enough to cover the seat. Owing to the scarcity of old English needlework to-day, a number of chairs and couches have been upholstered in eighteenth-century Dutch needlework, which is generally in the coarse stitch, with a disjointed floral design of small birds and figures ; the colouring is bad, bright reds and blues predominating, with none of the attractive harmonious colourings of the English.

Beside the much-restored and the extended needlework covering, a very large quantity of *gros* and *petit point* needlework, reproduced from the old, is made at the present day ; and this is used for upholstering not only spurious but genuine examples. It differs from the old needlework in its colouring ; the imitator, in order to produce an appearance of age, uses silks which are specially dyed to match the colours of the old work. He is unconcerned by the probability that his modern needlework will fade ; and, in consequence, after a short time, the colours made to match the old work have faded to a lighter tone. Old needlework is never found with the colourless appearance of the modern reproduction, in fact, in many genuine pieces, the colouring is quite fresh. There is also a difference in the drawing of the figures in an old piece, compared with the modern, especially noticeable in the faces and hands ; and the old needlework is hard and stiff, whereas the modern is soft and pliant.

Spurious examples of chairs, settees, couches, and stools are likely to be encountered, not only of entirely new construction, but genuine examples will be found with their value fictitiously increased by various devices.

One favourite expedient is to carve the ends of the arms of a plain chair with eagles' heads ; the corner chair is generally chosen for this deception, as the plain arm terminates in a round flat scroll which affords sufficient material for carving this feature. Owing to the rarity of the walnut armchair, the imitator uses the mahogany examples, of which a large number have survived. Although the commerical imitator makes sets of walnut hoop-back chairs and settees, his more skilled confrère confines his attention to the upholstered varieties of these articles, and has particularly favoured in the past the couch, chair, and stool with the lion mask. This type of fake has attained such notoriety that the market is no longer receptive, and the imitator has, consequently, turned his attention to earlier types, often using marquetry inlay instead of carving, as already mentioned.

Concerning the stool of this period, the collector must bear in mind the spurious example that, like that of the stool in the earlier period, has been made from the front legs of two single chairs. A pair of single chairs with upholstered backs were not so saleable in the past as one stool. The made-up stools of this period, of which many are about, can be detected, because the front leg of a chair is set at an acute angle, the front of the seat being wider than the back, while on a stool the legs are made at right angles. The chair legs when they are fitted on to a stool will, therefore, have the wings of the legs running under the seat-rail and will not line with the front edge of it. Stools should always be scrutinized for evidence of this deception, for while this adaptation is no longer feasible, owing to the scarcity of the genuine chairs, a number of such stools made in the past will be met with, generally of the type with the upholstery over the seat-rail, similar to Plate XVII (*a*).

The making of an upholstered-back couch from an upholstered-back arm-chair is another fraud that has been successfully carried out, judging from the number of spurious couches of this description that are to be found. The four legs and the arms of the chair will be utilized, the only visible part lacking being the middle front leg. This the imitator sometimes reproduces, whilst on other occasions he omits it altogether. Any couch or settee equal in width to two chairs, if genuine, will always have the centre front leg. Examples, therefore, without this leg are either spurious, or, if genuine, the leg has been damaged and lost ; in which case examination of the under-framing will show that it once existed.

To avoid the difficulty of the front leg the imitator often makes from a chair, the rare, small love-seat, which, as already described, has no centre leg ; but genuine seats of this description will have short legs similar to that of the winged arm-chair,* and not the taller leg of the chair or settee. Such examples of couches and love-seats should always be very carefully examined by the collector before purchasing. The exposed seat-rails will be of old beech, or, if made from modern, will be faked to give them an appearance of age. A useful test for these articles is, if possible, to examine the framework of the back and arms for any signs of the marks of the band- or circular-saw, for the imitator does not generally go to the trouble of removing all traces of such marks from the framework, which being covered by the upholstery will, in all probability, escape inspection.

A number of single chairs will be found converted into arm-chairs by the addition of spurious arms, as the arm-chair is not only more valuable than the single but far more saleable. To detect such a chair will not, however, require much circumspection, as owing to its narrow seat and back it will lack the proportions of the genuine arm-chair.

Many arm-chairs and stools which were originally made as night commodes have had the deep apron pieces of the seat-rails cut away, thus converting them into the ordinary specimens. The new stained and raw surface of the underside of the seat-rail will indicate that this conversion has been carried out.

The imitator in making chairs with the wooden splat back, will in most cases, to save expense, vary the construction of the shoe piece, which holds the splat in position on the back seat-rail, from that found on the genuine chair. The latter will have the splat and the shoe-piece separate, and the line where they join can be distinctly seen on examining the chair at the back. The imitator makes the seat-rail and shoe-piece in one, and to disguise the fact sometimes represents the join by a gouged line.

* The reason that the winged arm-chair, upholstered-back couch and love-seat have short legs is owing to their seats being fitted with squabs, and this increased height in the upholstery necessitated a reduction in the height of the leg.

PLATE XXXVIII

Collection of Frank Partridge

A bureau writing-cabinet decorated with English green and gold lacquer with bevelled mirror plates in doors surmounted by double-domed top, circa 1715.

Tables

The popular type of oblong table of the seventeenth century appears to have declined in favour in this half of the walnut period. A type of table that has survived from this latter half, and somewhat resembles the earlier oblong table, is that with a drawer in one side and round legs terminating in club-feet. The folding-top table, also met with, has similar legs. Both these types, however, exist in such small numbers that they could not have been as popular as the earlier oblong table.

In the reign of William III, the table known as the side table was introduced, but as the early specimens of this type, sometimes with scroll legs or heavy tapered legs,* connected by stretchers, are known, to-day, by only a few surviving examples, consideration of these tables has been deferred until this chapter.

The early eighteenth-century examples are small in size, with cabriole legs ending in either the club, the spade, or the claw-and-ball foot. Such small examples will be found in walnut; but the larger type of this table, which was a very popular piece of furniture from 1725 to 1750, will be met with in mahogany, and but seldom in walnut. A very rare side-table of large size is illustrated, Plate XXIII (*b*); the type of leg on this table is sometimes found on chairs and stools, and would appear to date about 1720. The early side tables of the reigns of William and Mary and Queen Anne had wooden veneered tops, whereas those from the reign of George I onwards had marble tops.† The earlier marble tops had their edges moulded, unlike the later tops, which had the edges square in section.

The oval gate-legged table in this period had developed into the table with the oval top and cabriole legs. Such tables, however, like the gate-legged tables, are hardly ever met with in walnut. Early examples with a carved shell on the knee, dating about 1720, or even earlier, were made of mahogany. With the exception of the oblong table, the other variety with the folding-top and the side table, no other walnut tables of this period appear to have been made in any quantity.

* An interesting side table with scroll legs and veneered walnut top, dating from the last years of the seventeenth century, is to be seen in the Royal apartments at Hampton Court. An unusual feature of this table is that the scroll legs, which are made of soft wood, are painted and grained in imitation of walnut. An analogous expedient to accentuate poorly marked and figured walnut veneer was to represent the markings by dark painted lines.

† Tables with marble tops could not have been unknown in the reign of William III, as Celia Fiennes, in her diary, *Through England on a Side Saddle*, mentions that at Hampton Court she saw two marble tables. These, presumably, were tables with marble tops on wooden stands; but whether the latter were walnut or gilt, English or Foreign, it is impossible to conjecture. Judging from existing examples, however, the table with marble top does not appear to have come into general use until the time mentioned.

PLATE XXXIX

Collection of Sir William Plender, G. B. E.

A bureau writing-cabinet, of Oriental workmanship, decorated with black and gold lacquer, circa 1730.

Card Tables

In the early years of the eighteenth century the turned and tapered legs of the circular folding-top card table of the William and Mary period were superseded by slender cabriole legs ending in spade-feet, and the stretchers were also discarded. The next type of card table was designed with a square top with projecting circular corners. The top overhung the frieze by two or three inches, and the legs were slender and cabriole, ending in club-feet. The four corners of the open top were made with circular sunk compartments for candlesticks, and shallow wells for counters were also fitted. By about 1720 the cabriole legs of this table became bolder; and the frame of the table was made larger, so that the projection of the top over the frieze was reduced (see example illustrated, Plate XXXI (*b*)). In these later tables the front corners of the frieze were circular, following out the shape of the top, whereas in the Queen Anne examples they were square.

Of this type of card table a number of fine-quality examples have survived, the legs ending in claw-and-ball or lion-paw feet, and the knees being carved with one of the various *motifs* already described. By about 1735 the design of the card table underwent a further change, the top now having square corners in place of the earlier circular ones. On these tops the compartments for the candlesticks are square and not circular. The "square-corner" card table is but seldom found in walnut, as it was introduced at too late a date for many examples to be made from this wood. The example, illustrated, Plate XXXII, of about 1735, has a serpentine front, which was another new feature introduced about this time, and which became extremely popular in the furniture of the latter half of the eighteenth century.

The folding leaf in these card tables is generally supported by one of the back legs, which is hinged on to the framework; but in some cases the leaf is upheld by two legs so that the top, when open, has a leg under each corner; and this arrangement, which is known as the "concertina," adds both interest and value to an example. A table with cabriole front legs, ending in claw-and-ball feet, also has an additional value if the back legs have the same termination. In the majority of such card tables the back legs have the club-foot.

Another rare type of folding-top card table, of which a few examples have survived, is one with a triangular-shaped top with a leg at each corner, and a fourth leg at the back which swings out to support the hinged leaf, the top, when opened, forming a square. The legs of this table are triangular in section and slightly cabriole. This type of table would appear

PLATE XL

Collection of Sir John Prestige

(Left) A bracket clock in case, overlaid with burr walnut veneer; movement by William Webster, Exchange Alley, London, circa 1730.

Collection of Sir John Prestige

(Right) A bracket clock in case, overlaid with burr walnut veneer; movement by William Webster, Exchange Alley, London, circa 1730.

to date from the latter years of Queen Anne's reign, and was made in both small and large sizes.

Although the majority of the card tables of this period appear to have been made in the standard size of about 3 feet in width, a few have survived of smaller dimensions, and these, owing to their rarity to-day, are more highly prized. Sometimes these tables will be found with veneered tops instead of the top covered with material ; such examples were presumably made for occasional tables in a room and not for card playing. Originally, it would appear to have been the fashion to make many of these card tables in pairs, as a number of pairs, both in walnut and mahogany, have survived ; in such cases, the value to-day of a pair of tables is more than double that of a single example.

The original covering to the top of a walnut card table was usually of velvet, which was pasted on to the top, and framed on the edges with narrow metal braid held in place by small brass-headed nails. The green baize top was not introduced until later in the eighteenth century. Besides the velvet it was the fashion to line the top of the card table with needlework, and a few rare examples with this covering have survived.

The collector will find that the genuine walnut card table which has not been French polished is by no means an easy piece to find ; and this is true not only of the more ornate examples with claw-and-ball feet, but also of the earlier, plainer type. He is much more likely to meet with mahogany examples, which exist to-day in far larger numbers.

Bureaux and Bureau-Bookcases

The introduction of the bureau-with-drawers in the reign of William and Mary has already been noted in Chapter IV. From the design of the earlier bureaux of this type they would not appear to be of a date prior to 1690, and such early examples dating from William the Third's reign are to-day of distinct rarity compared with the very large number that have survived from the first forty-five years of the eighteenth century. The bureau of the late seventeenth century differs in several features from that of the eighteenth century. The earliest examples of the former have the bureau wider than the base with drawers, as the bureau will be found to overhang the sides of the base by an inch or two. An example of this can be seen in the small bureau-on-stand, Plate XXVII (*a*). This feature seems to be peculiar to the seventeenth-century bureau, as it is not found on those of the early eighteenth century. Another feature of the seventeenth-century example is that the bureau and the base with drawers are in separate parts. In the later bureau of the Queen Anne period they were in one,

PLATE XLI

Metropolitan Museum of Art

American Cromwellian Chairs, circa 1690

(Left) Leather upholstered side chair. (Center) New England hardwoods side chair with original turkey work. (Right) beech armchair, spiral turnings like those used in England.

although an early example will still retain the moulding between the base and the bureau which originated to hide the join between the two (see Plate XXXVIII). The majority of the bureaux-with-drawers will be found about 3 feet to 3 feet 6 inches in width, whereas rarer and smaller examples will measure about 2 feet to 2 feet 6 inches.

The walnut bureau-bookcase, that is, the bureau-with-drawers surmounted by a bookcase with folding doors, has survived also in large numbers, although not to the same extent as the bureau. The bureau-bookcase will also be found with the two early features already described in the bureau. The designs for the treatment of the cornice to the upper part were varied. Some examples have a straight cornice similar to Plate XXIV, whilst other examples have a double-dome top, Plate XXXVIII, or a shaped curved top, similar to Plate XXXIX. Others, again, are found with a broken-arch pediment top, and another design, although extremely rare in walnut pieces, is the swan-neck pediment, similar to Plate XXV.

A favourite method of decorating the panels in the doors of the bookcase was with mirrors, for many such examples have survived ; but lower quality and cheaper examples had walnut panels that were much less costly than the mirror plates. The tops of the panels of the doors followed out the design of the cornice, as examples with the straight cornice will have oblong panels, and examples with the dome cornice will have the panels shaped similar to the example illustrated. Like the bureaux, these bureau-bookcases were made in two sizes, the majority 3 feet to 3 feet 6 inches, and a smaller size ranging from 2 feet or under to 2 feet 6 inches. Most of the smaller variety had one door in the top part, similar to example, Plate XXV, although a number have survived with two doors, similar to the larger examples. A feature which is unusual both in the bureau and the bureau-bookcase is for the base to be fitted with a pedestal with small drawers on each side and a cupboard in the recess, similar to example illustrated, Plate XXIV. Another unusual feature, mainly confined to the bureau-bookcase, is for the base to have cupboards instead of drawers. The early bureau-bookcases generally have their doors hung with the centre-pin hinge and not with the butt hinge. Sometimes examples are met with having brass butterfly hinges with shaped and engraved leaves.

The collector who is desirous of buying either of these two pieces will not encounter any difficulty in finding genuine specimens, but he should make his selection from those which have good patina and quality. The latter will be determined, to a large extent, by the presence of burr walnut veneer instead of the more usual straight-cut variety. The linings of the drawers should be of oak and the top edges of the sides of the drawers should be rounded and carefully finished off. The back of the drawer

PLATE XLII

Metropolitan Museum of Art

American Carved High-back Chairs

(Left) New England armchair, carved back crest, front stretchers, arms, and Spanish feet. (Right) Turned side chair, back crest and front stretcher carved in Flemish scrolls. Both made circa 1690.

front should also be of oak and not deal. Specimens with mirror plates in the panels of the doors are much more desirable than those with the walnut panels ; but it is essential that the mirror plates should be the original ones, as a number of bureau-bookcases will be found with new plates, especially the smaller type with a single door. The old plate can be recognized by its shallow bevelling and dark reflection, and the plate itself will be thin and not thick, as in the modern glass. To judge whether glass is thick or thin, if a coin or other object is placed touching the glass, the distance between it and its reflection on the mercury at the back will denote the thickness of the plate. The modern mirror plate will not only be much thicker and its reflection whiter, but the surface of the bevelling when viewed at an angle will show distinctly the marks or scratches of the emery wheel across the bevel. In the original bevel which will have been worked by hand, no such marks will be perceptible. The imitator is not able to obtain the dark reflection on his new mirror plate because he cannot make the glass a dark colour, as it is the glass itself that gives the dark reflection, and not the mercury on the back. Another point of difference is that the old mirror plates have silvered backs, whereas the modern have painted backs. Not only does the imitator replace the broken mirrors in the genuine bureau-bookcase, but he will, to enhance the value of those with wooden panels, substitute mirror plates for the wooden panels. Many bureau-bookcases will be found to-day with the silvering removed from the mirror plate, so that the top part can be used as a china cabinet. Such a procedure destroys the appearance of the piece, as a plain sheet of glass breaks up the design and is not in good taste. A few very rare bureau-bookcases have survived with plain glass instead of mirrors, and such an example is illustrated in Plate XXIV. In this case it will be noted that the door panel is formed into two portions by a cross-bar, the original designer recognizing how injurious to the proportion of the piece it would be if the panel was not divided.

The bureau-bookcase or bureau is not an article which the imitator has paid much attention to ; he does not make spurious imitations of new construction owing to the quantity of genuine examples that have survived. He has, however, been known to surmount a bureau with a top part which he has come across separated from its original bureau. In order to carry out this adaptation he will have to remove the walnut veneer from the top of the bureau ; and he will, also, have to surround its front edge and two sides with a cross-banded moulding, within which the top part will rest. One test that shows this adaptation to have been carried out is the presence of worm burrows along the surface of the deal top. The worm works in the interior and not on the surface of a piece of wood, and

Harvard Tercentenary Loan Exhibition 1936
Formerly Philip Flayderman
Formerly Philip Flayderman

PLATE XLIII

Three Pedigreed High-back Chairs

(Left) New England hard wood side chair, made 1705 by the Reverend Edward Holyoke, Harvard president 1737-1769. (Center) Maple chair, circa 1710, once owned by John Hancock and used at his inauguration as first governor of Massachusetts. (Right) Side chair, circa 1710, originally owned by Sir William Pepperill of Kittery, Maine, only native American granted an English baronetcy.

if its borings are visible, it is due to their being revealed by the removal of the veneer that previously concealed them. These worm burrows are also accentuated because the imitator in planing down the deal top to eradicate the marks of the toothed plane, with which the carcases of all veneered furniture were scribed to give a key for the veneer, removes the outer surface of the wood, and discloses the borings.

Small Bureaux-on-Stands

One of the earliest examples of this piece is illustrated in Plate XXVII (*a*), and this specimen not only has the turned legs of the late Charles II period, but also the early feature of the overlapping bureau top.

In design, the legs of the stand of the bureau follows out that of the leg furniture already described. The round tapered leg, similar to those of the bureau illustrated, Plate XXVII (*b*), is about 1700, and one with the cabriole leg ending in the club-foot, Plate XXVIII (*a*), is about 1735. Other walnut bureaux are known with the claw-and-ball foot, and examples of a later date than 1735 are to be found generally in mahogany. In the early specimens the stand and the bureau were separate, whereas in the later bureaux they were in one; although it is not unusual to find mahogany examples in two parts similar to the early specimens. Judging from existing examples of this small bureau-on-stand, it would appear to be a piece that was specially favoured by the well-to-do, as lower-priced examples of inferior quality have not survived. The bureau-with-drawers and bureau-bookcase, on the contrary, are met with to-day in varying degrees of quality; showing that the cabinet-makers made these articles to suit the needs of their various customers.

Genuine specimens of this small bureau-on-stand are highly prized and much sought after, and, as already mentioned, a very large number of spurious ones have been made.

The secretaire with knee-hole and let-down front, similar to example illustrated, Plate XXXVI (*a*), is a piece that would appear to have been first made in the reign of William III, but examples later than 1725 do not appear to have survived. To-day, it is a piece that is not often encountered, and therefore could not have been made in anything like the numbers of the bureau or bureau-bookcase.

The knee-hole pedestal writing-table in walnut is a very rare piece of furniture at the present time, in fact, from the small number of such pieces that have survived it could be said that this table was hardly ever made up to the end of the walnut period; and the majority of the existing examples extant are in mahogany, and not in walnut. Several writing-tables similar

PLATE XLIV

Formerly Francis P. Garvan Collection
Formerly Francis P. Garvan Collection
Metropolitan Museum of Art

American Banister-back Chairs

(Left) New England armchair, 1715-1730, maple and ash. (Center) Cherry side chairs, Pennsylvania, circa 1710. (Right) Armchair, mostly of walnut, probably New England, circa 1700.

to the example illustrated, Plate XXIX, of very large dimensions, are extant, and these would not appear to be of an earlier date than 1725. They are not of very high quality like the contemporary mahogany examples, and were most probably made originally for libraries of large country houses. The small pedestal table (see Plate XXXIV (*a*)), with the walnut top, must not, however, be included amongst these writing-tables, as, not having a leather or velvet top, they were undoubtedly originally made as dressing-tables.

The scarcity throughout the walnut period of all pieces of furniture for writing, with the exception of the bureau-with-drawers, the bureau-bookcase, and, in a lesser degree, the writing-cabinet with fall-down front, is an indication that these three articles of furniture were the only pieces used to any great extent for the purpose ; in fact, from the large number of the bureaux and bureau-bookcases that have survived it would appear that very few households among the upper and middle classes were without one of these articles.

Walnut Cabinets and Bookcases

The plain type of walnut cabinet, generally measuring about 3 feet 6 inches in width, with glazed doors supported on base with cupboard, has survived from this half of the period. The doors are glazed with square panes separated by heavy moulded bars, similar to the top part of the bureau-bookcase, Plate XXIV. A few surviving cabinets of this type are plain, with straight tops and no elaborate features ; and such cabinets were most probably used for housing china or ornaments rather than books.

The walnut bookcases, of which a few are extant, are similar in design to the one illustrated, Plate XXX. Such examples have a low base, generally composed of drawers, with a tall upper part enclosed by two glazed doors. The later bookcase with wings, of the latter part of George the Second's reign, is generally known to-day by examples in mahogany and not in walnut.

The cabinet-with-doors, so favourite an article in the time of Charles II and William and Mary, as already mentioned, is not found in this half of the period. A piece with panelled doors on a base with drawers,* however, is met with, but this is higher than the former cabinets and was most probably the forerunner of the familiar mahogany wardrobe, which was made in large numbers from the middle of the eighteenth century. This piece is sometimes found with the top drawer in the base made into a secretaire, the back of the drawer being fitted with pigeon-holes and small drawers.

* The value of this piece has often been fictitiously enhanced by the addition of spurious marquetry.

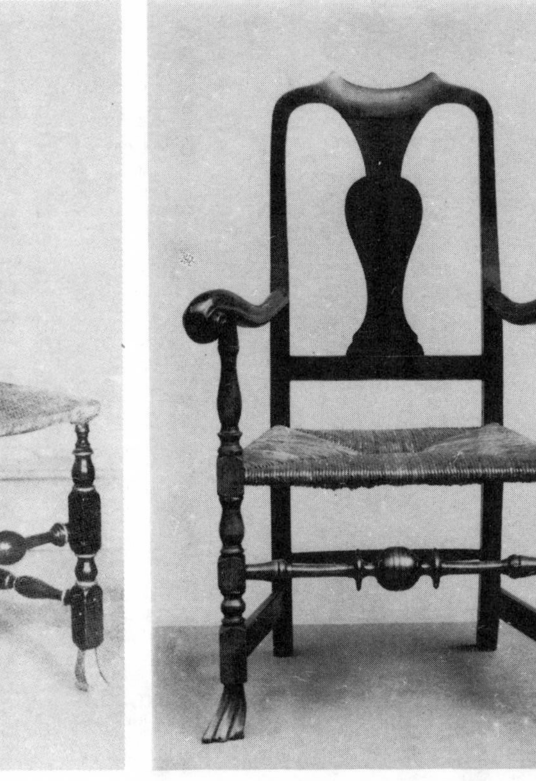

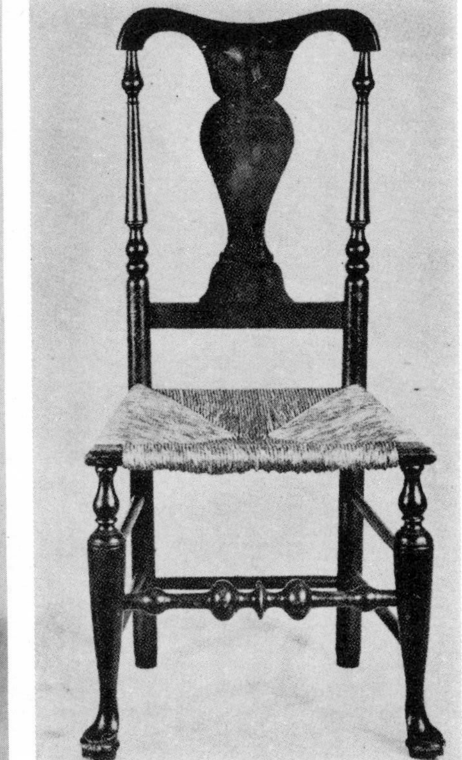

PLATE XLV

Formerly Francis P. Garvan Collection
Metropolitan Museum of Art
Anonymous

Early Vase-Splat American Chairs

(Left) Maple, painted to imitate walnut, turnings and feet in yellow. Southern New England, 1715-1725. (Center) Maple armchair with yoke-shaped cresting and carved arms, 1725-1730. (Right) Simple walnut side chair with pad feet, circa 1740.

Corner Cupboards

The corner-cupboard was an article that appears to have been first made in England in the early part of the eighteenth century, and examples dating up to 1730 are found in walnut. Such examples, which are very rare, have solid and not glazed doors. The tops are sometimes straight and sometimes decorated with a broken-arch pediment. The rarity of this piece of furniture in walnut is accounted for by the fact that corner-cupboards up to 1745 were generally fixtures in the room and made in deal with the wainscotting. Early examples in mahogany or walnut were not, therefore, often made. A type of Dutch walnut corner-cupboard with glazed doors, sometimes decorated with marquetry, must not be mistaken by the collector for an English specimen.

Chests-with-Drawers and Chests-on-Stands

The walnut chest-with-drawers was made in considerable numbers throughout the second half of the walnut period and even later. Examples are met with to-day in two sizes, the larger size 3 feet to 3 feet 6 inches, and the smaller size 2 feet to 2 feet 6 inches in width. The best examples are those with oak-lined drawers and decorated with burr walnut, the poorer quality having straight-cut veneer and deal linings. A number of foreign chests will be met with in this country, and these can generally be recognized by the fact that the side of the chest is decorated with a fielded panel, whereas the English examples have their sides plain.

The early chest-on-stand of this period is supported on slender cabriole legs, similar to the example illustrated, Plate XXXIII. Later chests have bolder legs, and sometimes have the knees decorated with an escallop shell. Very few examples have survived with claw-and-ball feet, as this piece of furniture was originally intended for a bedroom, and was not, therefore, a piece often made in an elaborate fashion. Generally, the chests have straight tops similar to the example illustrated, but more important specimens have survived with the broken-arch top. Some of the later examples will have the corners of the chest and stand canted and decorated with fluting; but this feature is unlikely to appear on a chest of a date prior to 1730.

As already mentioned these chests and chests-on-stands were made in walnut right up to 1745, and examples of the chest even later, and but few of them will be found in mahogany.

The dates of existing examples can be determined by the mouldings on or round the drawer fronts as in other drawer furniture of this period; and the remarks given in Chapter IV, concerning the legs to the stands, and the number that have had their patina destroyed by modern polishing, also

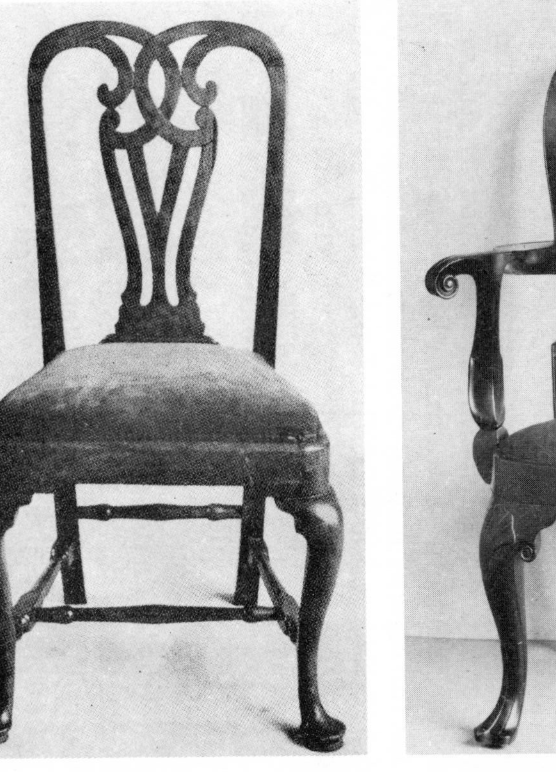

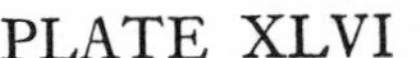

PLATE XLVI

Formerly Philip Flayderman
Formerly Howard Reifsnyder Collection
Ginsburg & Levy, Inc.

Fine American Queen Anne Chairs of Walnut

(Left) Side chair with double-arched crestings and pierced splat. (Center) William Savery labeled armchair. Has carved shells on cresting and knees of front legs, circa 1760. (Right) Side chair, modified splat, shaped stretchers, pad-footed cabriole legs, Philadelphia, 1755-1765.

refer to these eighteenth-century specimens. The variation in quality of both these articles is very noticeable, the earlier ones being usually of better quality than the later specimens. Many chests of poor quality will be found with the front only veneered and the sides formed by the carcase. The mouldings on the sides will also be worked in the solid and not cross-banded with walnut. Such pieces are of considerably less value now than those with the sides veneered and with cross-banded mouldings.

Tallboys or Double Chests

The tallboy or double chest was a piece introduced in the early years of the eighteenth century. The earlier and rarer specimens are lower than the later examples, and the cornice has a cushion frieze with drawer similar to that on the writing-cabinet, Plate XII. Later examples are taller and have canted corners decorated with fluting, as sometimes found on the chest-on-stand. A decorative feature also met with on the tallboy is that the bottom drawer and plinth moulding are shaped and decorated with a niche inlaid with a star design. Some tallboys, similar to the chests-on-stands, will have the broken-arch top, but these are far rarer than those with the straight top. The later chests dating from 1740 have the ogee bracket instead of the plain bracket foot, and examples with such feet are generally found with the corners of the front canted. Another feature, found in some of these pieces, is a slide on which to brush clothes, which is pulled out from the lower part just above the top drawer. In some cases the two portions of the tallboy will have become separated and will be found converted into separate chests-with-drawers. Such chests will have been fitted with plain, unveneered tops, and the chest formed from the top portion will have had a plinth and bracket feet added to it.

The notes just given concerning variations in quality of the chests-with-drawers and chests-on-stands also refer to tallboys.

Many tallboys, especially of the later type, have survived, but this piece of furniture is not considered so valuable as the chest-on-stand, not having the lightness in design of the latter article.

Dressing-Tables

The small dressing-tables on legs and the pedestal dressing-table, similar to the two examples illustrated, Plate XXXIV (*a* and *b*), have both survived in considerable numbers in walnut from this half of the period. As already mentioned neither of these articles are likely to be found of a greater width than 3 feet.

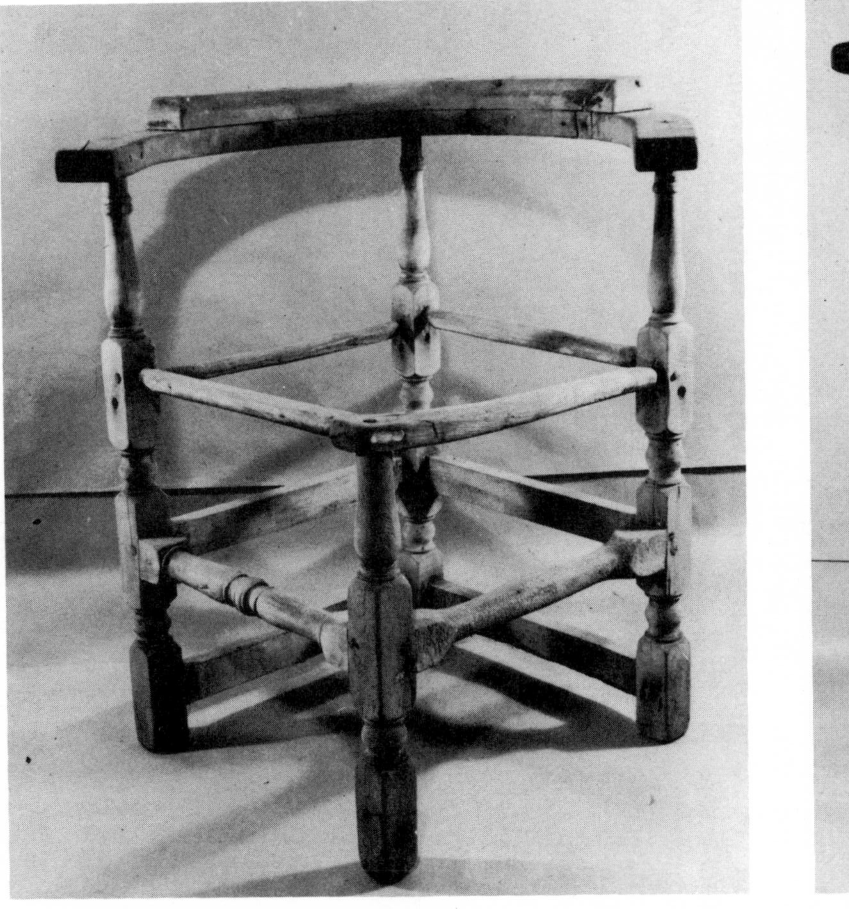

PLATE XLVII

Bruce Millar Collection

American Roundabout Chairs

(Left) Rush seat removed to show simplicity of structure. Original ball feet have disappeared. New England, maple, circa 1725. (Right) New England Queen Anne maple chair, 1730-1740. Front leg cabriole and pad footed.

Like the legs of the chairs, the legs of the former table altered in design throughout this period, the earlier examples having slender cabriole legs, and the later the bolder cabriole, sometimes ending in a claw-and-ball foot similar to the rare specimen illustrated. The majority of these dressing-tables, however, are not likely to be found with legs of such an elaborate character, generally having the plain cabriole, ending in the club-foot, and, if ornamented at all, usually with a shell on the knee. As already mentioned, both these types of tables were undoubtedly intended for dressing-tables and not for writing-tables, as none of them originally had the top covered in velvet or leather. Examples with such tops have been converted at a later date to make them more convenient for use as writing-tables.

Owing to their small size and inconvenience either as writing or dressing-tables, and also to the number that have survived, these tables are not very highly esteemed to-day, unless they have some unusual or ornate feature.

Both these tables will be found in mahogany, especially the pedestal table, but these, like the other plain contemporary furniture in this wood, do not compare in decorative value with the walnut specimens.

Owing to the absence of a genuine walnut dressing-table of convenient size, the imitator has supplied the want by a fictitious example made from the stand of a chest-with-drawers. He veneers the top ; but, as already noted, the original legs of these stands being generally missing, he supplies new legs of an elaborate character, also cutting away the shaped apron-piece under the centre drawer to give space for the knees of the user. So much of this converted stand is modern that the collector should not have much difficulty in recognizing the imitator's handiwork ; but he should in any case be wary of dressing-tables on legs which measure more than 3 feet in width, as it is highly improbable that they are genuine.

Tripod Furniture

The tripod table of the late seventeenth century developed in the eighteenth century into one similar to the example shown,* of about 1735, Plate XXVIII (*b*). This type of table with tripod foot must have become very fashionable in the second quarter of the eighteenth century, as many examples, both plain and decorated, have survived. Tables in walnut of this type, whether plain or decorated, however, could have been but seldom made, the cabinet-maker perhaps being deterred, as with the gate-leg table,

* Between these two varieties, however, there is a transitional type still retaining the scroll leg of the earlier tripod foot. Very few of these large tripod tables with scroll legs have survived, although Hogarth portrays several such tables in his pictures. These were most probably mahogany examples and not walnut.

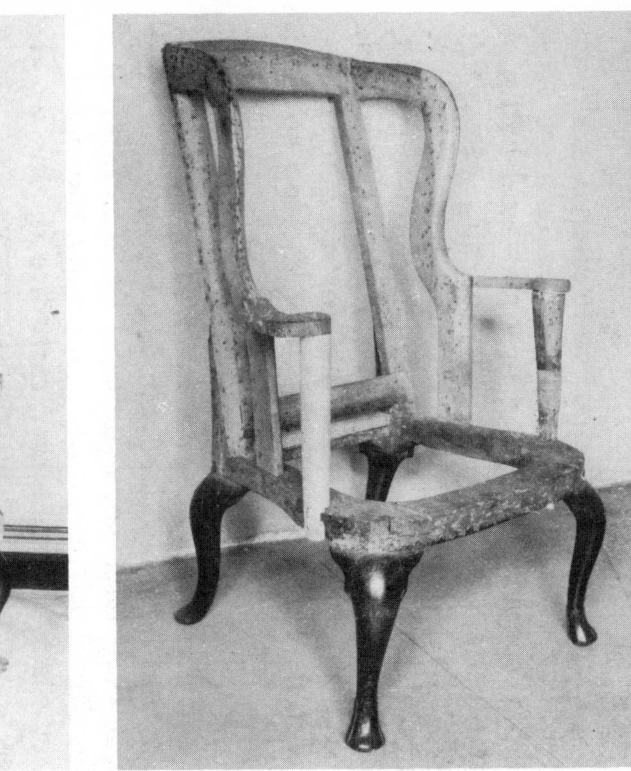

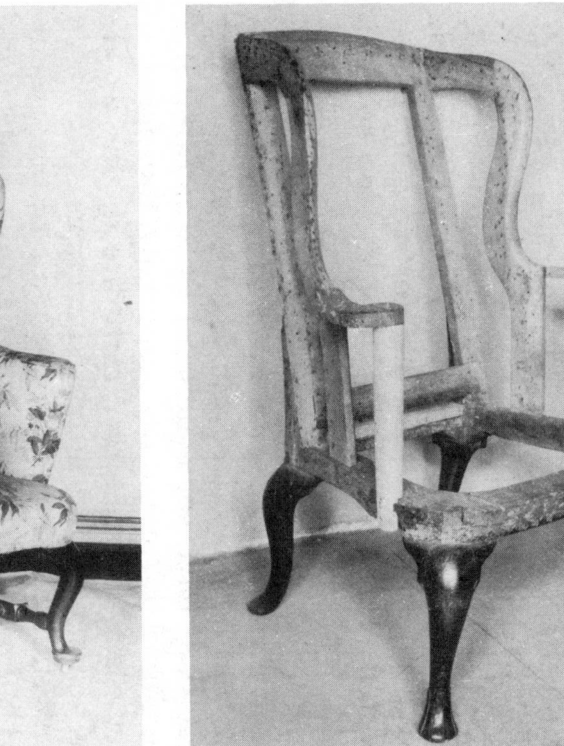

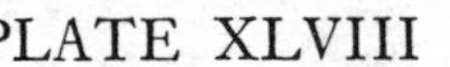

PLATE XLVIII

Metropolitan Museum of Art
Ginsburg & Levy, Inc.
Ginsburg & Levy, Inc.

American Wing Chairs

(Left) Has front feet and stretchers of walnut, back legs of maple. New England, circa 1725. (Center) Legs and stretchers of walnut, Philadelphia, circa 1740. (Right) Frame stripped of upholstery to show construction. Omission of stretchers indicates Georgian influence. Philadelphia, circa 1750.

by the difficulty of obtaining sufficiently large planks of walnut, after the sap wood had been cut away, to form a top of any size. The making of a solid walnut top in several pieces would not be satisfactory, as owing to the nature of the walnut wood it was liable to warp and split. This has happened to the walnut top of the example shown, as to prevent warping it was glued down on an oak foundation, now the only part of the top remaining.

In the mahogany examples this difficulty would not occur, as sufficiently large pieces of mahogany could be obtained to turn the top out in one piece.

The tops of the more important mahogany examples were sometimes decorated with the familiar pie-crust edge, but the cheaper tables had the edge either finished with a turned rim or left quite plain.

Besides this tripod table a type of tall stand with tripod foot was made, presumably, to hold candlesticks. These stands, generally measuring 4 feet to 4 feet 6 inches in height, had gallery tops to retain the candlestick in its place, and the stem was decorated with turning and sometimes fluting, similar to the tables. Examples of these in walnut are, however, of extreme rarity, and the majority of existing specimens, which date from 1730 to the end of the period and later, will be found in mahogany. These candlestands, often met with in pairs, are very highly valued and much sought after. Spurious examples are generally in mahogany, and a certain number of them have had their carving enriched with gilding. This eighteenth century stand is taller than the earlier variety with twisted stem, already described and illustrated.

Fire Screens, Cheval and Tripod Pole Stands

The cheval fire screen of the type illustrated, Plate XXXV (*a*), was first made in the reign of William III. The early specimens usually have the cresting to the frame, containing the needlework panel, elaborately decorated with carved and pierced foliage. Such examples, however, are but seldom English, as they nearly always contain Dutch or Flemish panels of needlework, the English example of this type being much rarer. These screens of the eighteenth century are plain in design, similar to the example illustrated; the majority, however, are generally in mahogany. Many spurious screens of the early elaborate type have been made within recent years by the imitator, who mounts in the frames genuine panels of needlework.

The present-day value of the cheval screen depends to a great extent upon the fineness of the stitch of the needlework and also upon whether it is a floral or a figure subject, the latter, similar to the example illustrated, being by far the more valuable.

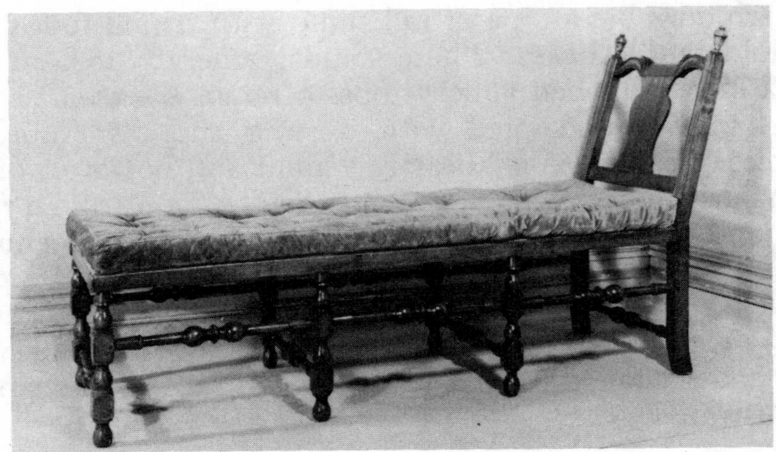

PLATE XLIX

Metropolitan Museum of Art
Ginsburg & Levy, Inc.
Metropolitan Museum of Art

Three American Day-beds

(Top) Stuart design, maple, circa 1690. (Center) Walnut, vase-turned legs, ball and ring turned stretchers, circa 1720. (Bottom) Curly maple, made by Job Townsend, Newport, Rhode Island, 1743.

All these screens were made so that the frame containing the needlework could be raised and lowered, it being made to run in grooves in the two side supports.

The tripod pole screen, similar to the tripod table, is but seldom found in walnut, the majority extant being in mahogany. Specimens in the latter wood, dating from about 1730 onwards, have survived in considerable numbers, both with the decorated tripod foot and stem, and also with the plain tripod foot. The earlier and rarer examples in walnut are generally smaller in the spread of the tripod foot, and have the knee of the leg carved with a shell, as example illustrated, Plate XXXV (*b*).

Many tripod stands of these pole screens have been transformed within recent times into tables. Such a conversion is easily recognized by the fact that the stand of a screen, being lower than that of a table, will have a piece added on to bring it up to table height. The stem of a tripod table, on the contrary, will always be in one piece ; and, if otherwise, it can be definitely assumed that it is a pole-stand converted.

Walnut Mirrors

The mirror with walnut frame does not appear to have been much favoured in the eighteenth century, being replaced, as already stated, by the more popular gilt-framed mirror. The most usual type of walnut mirror in the reign of Queen Anne and George I is tall and narrow, with shaped top and hood. The frames are sometimes of half-round section, or flat with moulded edges, and similar to the earlier mirrors ; many of this type have lost their hoods.

Besides this mirror, another type, dating from the reigns of George I and George II, has an architectural character, with swan-neck or broken pediment top, and shaped frame. The mouldings and ornamentation to the mirror are of gilt, but the frame will be found overlaid with either walnut or mahogany veneer, and more often with the latter.

The imitator does not pay much attention to walnut mirrors of this period, with the exception of the very rare overmantel mirror with a walnut frame. These mirrors were intended to rest on the chimneypiece, and were designed with a horizontal mirror divided into three plates surmounted by an oil-painting depicting a landscape or still-life subject. The genuine example is but seldom found ; but many imitations have been made, an old picture being utilized for the purpose.

Another type of overmantel mirror is one with three plates as described above, but without the decorative feature of the picture surmounting it. This mirror is but seldom found with a walnut frame, most examples being framed in a narrow gilt gesso moulding. Owing to their ready sale to-day, the imitator has made many spurious examples, sometimes of the type with projecting square corners, the mouldings being gilt, and the frame veneered with walnut.

Examination of the backs of these mirror frames will disclose the faked surface of the deal or pine, very unlike the mature surface of the genuine specimen. To hide the new wood the imitator will paint and coat it with dark stain and varnish; but if the surface is tested by an incision with a penknife, as described on page 45, the spurious nature of the piece will be disclosed. The remarks concerning the bevelling and the painted back of the new mirror plate given on page 135 should also be remembered.

Bedsteads

The upholstered bed of the previous period would appear to have remained in favour for the first twenty-five or thirty years of the eighteenth century. An example of an upholstered bed is portrayed in one of Hogarth's pictures of "Marriage à la mode."

When mahogany began to be used for furniture-making, this upholstered type was superseded by the mahogany bedstead, with plain, fluted front posts; the latter again becoming a decorative feature, as they had been in the earlier oak beds.

These early mahogany four-post bedsteads, however, still retained the shaped and moulded cornice to the tester top covered with the upholstering fabric like the previous bedstead. The posts of the mahogany bedsteads grew more elaborate in design until about 1750, when the cornices are sometimes found in mahogany with carved ornament, instead of the earlier covered examples.

There is no record of a genuine bedstead with walnut posts, the walnut wood going out of fashion before the bedstead with carved posts came into vogue.

CHAPTER VII

LACQUER FURNITURE

1660–1730

IN the England of Elizabethan times, Oriental products were not unknown, both the Dutch and English East India Companies having been formed in this reign; and such articles of Oriental manufacture as Chinese cabinets, carpets, screens, and embroideries figure in late sixteenth and early seventeenth-century inventories. Both Holland and Portugal were largely interested in the Eastern trade, the volume of which greatly increased during the seventeenth century, and a new vogue for things Oriental influenced both France and Holland in the latter half of the century. On the accession of Charles II this Oriental taste spread to England under the auspices of the Court; a part of the dowry of the Queen, Catherine of Braganza, consisted of "Indian" cabinets, porcelain, and fabrics. In those days the products of the East were termed "Indian."

The king and his brother, the Duke of York, also owned "Indian" cabinets, which are referred to by Evelyn and Pepys; and both these celebrated diarists make mention of "Indian" pieces in houses that they visited, which shows that at this period Oriental products were sufficiently uncommon as to call for special notice.

These "Indian" cabinets and screens were of lacquer, and after their introduction into English Court circles, lacquer ware began to be imported into England in considerable quantity. To meet the increasing demand for lacquer furniture, designs of European pieces were sent out to the East, so that the Chinese and Japanese could make their lacquer furniture on the lines of the European. The vogue for Eastern lacquer also induced the European cabinet-makers to start making lacquer in imitation of the Oriental product. The lacquer work executed in England was called "Japanning," and became so popular that it was not only made commercially, but developed into a fashionable pastime; and for the guidance of interested amateurs, *A Treatise of Japanning and Varnishing* was published in 1688 by Stalker and Parker, which gave many recipes and designs for carrying out "japan" work.

The importation of " Indian " lacquered furniture by the merchants in the late seventeenth century seriously affected the trade of the European manufacturers; and caused an outcry amongst the artisans of Holland, France, and England for laws to protect the native industries, although it was admitted at the time that the Oriental lacquer work was far superior to any that was produced in Europe.

The lacquer imported into England from the East can be divided, roughly, into two varieties, one similar to that illustrated, Plate XXXIX, on which the ornament was raised in parts; and the other, called incised or cut lacquer, in which the design was cut in the surface and afterwards decorated with colours. The Oriental lacquer has a hard, lustrous surface, being made from the resin of gum trees, whereas the European substitute was more in the nature of paint and varnish.

The supply of designs for English pieces to the Oriental makers, and the making of " japanned " furniture in England, led to the decoration with lacquer of many other articles besides the Oriental cabinet and screen; in fact, it is probable that every article that was made in walnut was also made in English lacquer. In addition to furniture, the wainscotting of rooms was also decorated with lacquer.*

The lacquer furniture of English production was identical in every way to the walnut examples, the carcase being made of deal or oak, as already described. Many of the best quality pieces appear to have been veneered before they were lacquered. This was done to obtain a smoother and better surface† and to cover up the joins of the carcase, which, through shrinkage, would open and cause the lacquer to crack. When covered with veneer the risk of cracking would be considerably lessened, and would only occur if the veneer, itself, split. A number of veneered walnut pieces were undoubtedly lacquered at a later date in the eighteenth century; and this would also account for a number of examples having veneer under the lacquer. But as lacquered cabinets, which were not made in the walnut wood, are found veneered, this tends to prove that the carcase of high quality pieces, specially made for lacquering, were first overlaid with veneer. The mouldings of such pieces are in the solid and not cross-banded, as they would be on walnut pieces that were lacquered at a subsequent date.

The pieces of Oriental manufacture, although similar in design and

* Celia Fiennes records in her diary (*temp*. William and Mary) that at Burghley House, Stamford, the seat of Lord Exeter, " My Lady's Closet is very ffine, the wanscoate of the best Jappan."

† In deal and oak, the shrinkage of the softer fibres between the harder year rings results in the latter standing out, and this feature will be seen on many pieces which have been lacquered direct on the carcase without veneering.

form to the English, varied in the smaller details, and especially in the execution of the cabinet work ; the dovetails were very coarse, and, in some cases, where they were omitted, the sides of the drawers were held together with wooden pegs. The mounts were also much thinner than on the English examples, and were sometimes of Oriental design, as seen on the example illustrated, Plate XXXIX.

Both the exterior and interior of the drawer linings will be found painted in the Oriental pieces, whereas in the best English examples, in which the drawer-linings were of oak, the insides of the drawers only were painted, generally a dull red and sprinkled with gold. On the poor quality English pieces, made with deal linings, both the interiors and the exteriors of the drawers were usually painted, similar to the Oriental examples.

Although a very large quantity of furniture of Oriental make must have been imported into England in the late seventeenth century, a much larger quantity of the English "japanned" work has survived. Like the existing walnut furniture, the greater part of the lacquer furniture dates rom the first twenty-five or thirty years of the eighteenth century, as the examples of seventeenth-century lacquer extant are mostly confined to the cabinets-with-doors mounted on stands. This type of cabinet was undoubtedly the earliest piece to be imported into England from the East in the reign of Charles II ; and it appears, also, to be the earliest piece that was made in the English "japan."

Judging from the lacquer furniture extant, certain articles have survived in far larger numbers than others ; for instance, many square cabinets-with-doors and long-case clocks are in existence. The reason for the survival of so many clock-cases, however, is attributable to the fact that, while lacquer furniture went out of vogue about 1730, the use of lacquer for decorating clock-cases continued up to the end of the century. In this respect they are analogous to the marquetry clock-cases, which, as already mentioned, continued to be made for ten or fifteen years after marquetry furniture had declined in favour.

Owing to the perishable nature of lacquer furniture, the amount that has survived can only be a small part of what was originally made ; and the fact that some articles exist to-day in larger numbers than others is due to the nature of such pieces being better fitted to withstand the wear of time and use.

The Oriental lacquer furniture also shows a preponderance of certain articles ; for instance, the cabinet, the bureau-bookcase, and the chest with domed lid, have survived in larger numbers than other pieces. The long-case clock in Oriental lacquer is practically unknown. The incised or cut lacquer, as found to-day, is generally confined to screens, to cabinets mounted

PLATE L

Formerly Helen Temple Cook Collection
Metropolitan Museum of Art

Rare American Settees

(Top) Queen Anne two-chair-back settee. Walnut, circa 1740. (Bottom) Upholstered sofa settee, Philadelphia, circa 1750; made for Governor James Logan of Pennsylvania.

on stands, and to chests. Many of the two latter articles have been made from incised lacquer screens, as the panels on the doors and sides do not contain a complete design. Besides cabinets and chests, a few rare tables, mirror frames, and other articles of furniture have also survived made from panels obtained from the coromandel screens ; in fact, the majority of incised pieces extant would appear to have been formed in this manner, as but few will be found with panels specially made for the articles which they decorate. Such pieces were made in England from the imported screens.

Lacquer decoration on English furniture was carried out with various coloured backgrounds, by far the most favoured being the black, as the majority of the surviving pieces have the background of this colour. More valuable pieces, however, are those with the red ground, as such examples are not only of far more decorative value, but are extremely scarce. Pieces of lacquer with blue and green backgrounds have also survived, the blue perhaps being the rarer of the two ; but the rarest of all the colours is the cream or pale yellow, and only a few pieces are known to exist with this rare ground. Both the Oriental and English lacquer declined in favour about 1730 ; the incised lacquer variety, however, appears never to have been very popular in England, and the majority of the cabinets, screens and chests with this lacquer that have survived would appear to date from the seventeenth rather than the eighteenth century.

Lacquer furniture would seem, from existing examples of it, to have been specially favoured for use in bedrooms, which in the early eighteenth century were often decorated in the Chinese taste, the walls sometimes being hung with papers of Oriental design. About 1750 lacquer again came into favour, which fact can be gathered from the published designs of the cabinet-makers of that period, as many examples are given which it is suggested would look well if treated with "japan." The majority of these later designs were also for pieces of bedroom furniture. Many more examples of the earlier lacquer have survived, however, than of this middle eighteenth-century revival ; and, as this later variety is outside the walnut period, it does not come within the purview of this book.

The present-day condition of the majority of old lacquer pieces shows them to be in varying states of disrepair, for lacquer, unlike walnut, has not improved by age ; use and wear having the effect of denting and scratching the surface and wearing off the gilding from the raised portions of the design. This scratching and denting of the surface, however, is more general on the softer English lacquer than on the harder surface of the Oriental ; but the latter, owing to this very quality of hardness, has a tendency to crack and chip off in a manner similar to veneer, in addition to

PLATE LI

Formerly Erastus T. Taft Collection
Ginsburg & Levy, Inc.

Early Small Tables

(Top) American Cromwellian table. Maple and oak, New England, circa 1680. (Bottom) Small table with oval top. Legs and central stretcher, cup, trumpet and ball-turned. Pennsylvania, before 1710.

which the colours of the design sink in, and the gold wears off. The incised or cut lacquer has stood the wear of age better than the other two varieties.

A large quantity of the English lacquer has also been ruined through its surface being coated with a thick opaque varnish, which in some cases has entirely hidden the design ; in fact, on some pieces only the raised portions are now to be seen. This varnishing of old pieces, probably for the purpose of renovation, appears to have been confined to the English examples, as the highly polished surface of the Oriental would not be improved by such treatment.

The decorative value of those pieces, both of Oriental and English lacquer, which have their gilt design standing out in brilliant contrast to the darker background, is markedly superior to the worn or varnished example which has only the merit of age to recommend it. In the former piece, the patches of colour used in the design will add their quota to the decorative effect, whereas in the varnished example the colours will not be distinguishable. Many pieces which, originally, had a blue or green ground have been so heavily varnished in recent years that the background now appears to be black ; and it is owing to this pernicious practice, in the past, of renovating lacquer with thick mastic varnish that the brilliant piece is so scarce at the present time.

Besides the varnished example, many English pieces are extant with their surfaces much restored. In some cases this has been done so well that it is only by very careful examination that the restored parts can be discerned. The Oriental pieces with the raised design are not so often found restored owing to the difficulty of imitating this type of lacquer, which, as already stated, varies considerably from the English variety.

Apart from the difficulty of finding a piece in brilliant condition, the collector will have to contend with a very large quantity of spurious lacquer that has been made ; and it is no exaggeration to say that more than two-thirds of the lacquer furniture sold as antique is fraudulent. This, however, refers to the English lacquer, as the Oriental variety with the raised design is not imitated. The incised or cut lacquer, which it is possible to reproduce, as described later, has also received its share of attention from the imitator.

Just as there are degrees of quality in fraudulent walnut examples, so there are similar degrees in the spurious lacquer, the pieces made by the commercial imitator having by no means the same resemblance to the old example as those made by the skilled faker. In fact, the productions of the former are generally offered to the public under the guise of "an old but not period" piece ; and by this rather subtle description a better price is more readily obtained for them than if they were described as of new manufacture. The skilled faker of old lacquer, however, has more confidence in his wares, and proclaims them to be genuine specimens of the reign of Queen Anne, and the prices he obtains are, in consequence, considerably higher.

This variation in spurious lacquer is specially noticeable in regard to the gilding. In poor work the gold design will be made with bronze powder, whereas in the high quality work gold leaf will be employed. The dullness of the former in comparison to the transparent brilliance of the latter is specially noticeable; for the bronze powder has not the lasting properties of the real gold, which improves by age. The deep rich colour of the gold on the old piece is attributable to the thin varnish with which the lacquer surface was originally finished. The mellowing of this varnish by long exposure to the atmosphere gives to the gold the same rich, translucent effect that it gives to the walnut wood. The imitator also finishes his piece with varnish, and this will produce in time the same effect as it has done on the old piece.

The surface of the old lacquer, both of the background and the raised, gilded portions of the design, will be found to have a network of fine hair cracks. The imitator, however, to obtain, immediately, an appearance of age, cracks the surface of his lacquer artificially by applying a paste over it; and the contraction of this paste in drying cracks the varnish with which the lacquer has been coated. This artificial method of cracking the lacquer surface makes cracks of quite a different nature to those found on a genuine piece. The cracks on the latter, if closely examined, will seem to extend not only through the varnish but also the coating of lacquer; but on the spurious piece the varnish on the top of the lacquer only is affected. The artificial cracks, moreover, are large; in fact, very similar to those sometimes found on old oil paintings which have been heavily varnished. The collector who is desirous of purchasing only genuine pieces should make himself familiar with the cracking of the spurious piece, as this knowledge will stand him in good stead when determining the authenticity of an example.

Besides the artificial cracking of the spurious example, the surface of the lacquer will be soft, very unlike the hard and dry surface of the genuine piece. It will take a number of years for the modern lacquer to harden, and examples of recent manufacture, therefore, can be tested in this respect.

The surface of a genuine lacquer piece will also show signs of wear. For instance, on the flap of a bureau, or a cupboard door that has been constantly handled, the lacquer will have worn off and, in some cases, shows the wooden carcase underneath. The raised portions of the design, which are usually gilt, will have the gilding worn away, disclosing the white composition of which these raised parts are formed. This wearing away of the

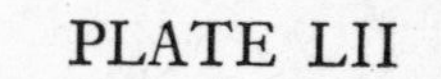

PLATE LII

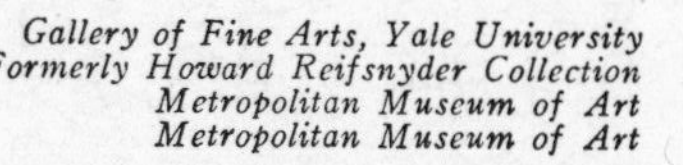

Gallery of Fine Arts, Yale University
Formerly Howard Reifsnyder Collection
Metropolitan Museum of Art
Metropolitan Museum of Art

American Gate-leg Tables

(Top, left) Large walnut table with simple gates. Pennsylvania, circa 1720. (Bottom, left) Trestle table with block feet. Pennsylvania 1725-1750. (Top, right) Small table, circular top. Walnut, circa 1685. (Bottom, right) Very large with two gate supports for each leaf. Walnut, New England 1690-1725.

gilding will have occurred on those parts of the piece which have been dusted constantly, like the flap of a bureau, or the top of a table; the mouldings on the front of a piece, also, will have the lacquering and gilding more worn and rubbed than those on the sides. On the spurious example, however, the wearing of the gilding on the raised design will be general over the whole of the piece, as the imitator, to give it an antique appearance, treats every part in the same manner, and does not graduate the treatment according to the wear which each part would naturally receive. This question of the wear of the lacquer is a useful factor in determining whether a piece is genuine or not.

The imitator who sets out to deceive his customers does not usually make pieces of new construction, but will confine his efforts to lacquering old articles, as by this expedient, he saves himself the trouble of faking the carcase of a piece, and has only to treat the exterior lacquered surface. He will, for instance, take an old walnut chest-with-drawers or a secretaire with fall-down front, and strip off the old veneer, which he afterwards uses for veneering a spurious piece of walnut; and he then proceeds to lacquer the stripped carcase. This lacquering of old pieces he will carry out on any examples that he considers suitable for the purpose; and in the following notes, on various pieces of old lacquer furniture, mention will be made of those pieces of which spurious imitations are usually made by this method.

Cabinets

The cabinet and the coromandel screen are the earliest pieces of lacquer that have survived; the former both in the Oriental lacquer and in the English "japan." The early cabinets of the Charles II period, of Eastern manufacture, were mounted on stands after their arrival in this country, similar to the example illustrated, Plate I. The English cabinets were also mounted on similar stands, and from examples of both the Oriental and English cabinets extant there appear to be many more of the latter than of the former in existence. The Oriental cabinet is also found on an Oriental lacquer stand; but such cabinets are by no means to-day of such interest and value as the English examples. The stands altered in design according to the prevailing fashion, the early examples being decorated with cupids and figures amidst foliage, similar to the two specimens illustrated. Later examples, dating from the time of William and Mary, show the influence of "*le style refugié.*" Cabinets were also mounted in this reign on lacquered stands with turned legs connected by flat stretchers, similar to the stands of the chests-with-drawers. The Queen Anne cabinet was mounted on a stand with cabriole legs, generally "japanned," and the cabinets of the

PLATE LIII

Formerly Francis P. Garvan Collection
Formerly Francis P. Garvan Collection
Formerly Philip Flayderman
Israel Sack, Inc.

Butterfly Tables

(Top, left) Maple, with large butterfly supports, before 1720. (Bottom, left) "Tuckaway," turned trestle base and block feet. Maple throughout, retains original bluish-gray paint. Late seventeenth century. (Top, right) Oblong top, scalloped corners, curly maple, 1720-1730. (Bottom, right) Maple with original red paint. Connecticut, circa 1715.

George I period will be found on stands with the cabriole leg ending in the claw-and-ball foot; while other rare specimens of the early eighteenth century have survived with carved and gilt stands, having cabriole legs ending in claw-and-ball or lion-paw feet, and the knees of the legs sometimes decorated with masks. Another type of stand of this period is the one made of gilt gesso, usually with cabriole legs, on which the ornament is in low relief, carved out of composition laid on the wood.

The early stands of the Charles II and William and Mary periods were both gilt and silvered, but the latter process must have been more usual, as the majority of the finest seventeenth-century cabinets extant have the silvered stand. Sometimes a cabinet was mounted on a base-with-drawers, or a cupboard-with-doors, but neither of these pieces have the same decorative appearance as the example on stand.

The majority of the cabinets extant have the black ground, and a number have also survived with the red. The blue, green, and yellow grounds do not appear to have been favoured for the decoration of these cabinets, as genuine examples with these colours are but rarely met with; in fact, it is doubtful whether a genuine cabinet with a yellow or cream background is in existence. Some cabinets will also be found decorated with what is called tortoise-shell lacquer, in which the background is an imitation of tortoise-shell, being a dull red colour with dark markings. The design is in gold similar to the other types of lacquer.

The high value and rarity of the Charles II and William and Mary cabinets, on carved and silvered or gilt stands, has led to many spurious specimens being made by the imitator. These are sometimes of entirely new construction; but in other cases the imitator will re-lacquer genuine cabinets which, owing to their bad condition, are of little value.

The spurious lacquer cabinets of the imitator will usually be found with either a red, blue, green or yellow background, as he finds the cabinet with the black ground does not sell so readily. The rarity of the red lacquer cabinet, and the fact that cabinets with grounds in the other colours are practically unknown, should make the collector view with suspicion any supposed genuine example with these rare backgrounds that he may come across.

The genuine lacquer cabinet will usually have the doors cracked owing to the shrinkage of the carcase, and the interior of the cabinet will be brighter and fresher in colour than the exterior. This is particularly noticeable in the red lacquer examples, and if one of the hinges is removed from a cabinet of this description it will be seen that the red ground covered up by the hinge is very much brighter and fresher than the exposed surface surrounding it. In the spurious red lacquer cabinet these peculiarities will not be found,

PLATE LIV

Formerly Francis P. Garvan Collection
Yale University, Gallery of Fine Arts
Formerly Francis P. Garvan Collection

American Tavern Tables

(Top) Six-foot table with ball feet nearly worn away. Has large and small drawers with wooden knobs. Walnut, Pennsylvania, 1720-1735. (Bottom, left) Small walnut table, circa 1725. (Bottom, right) Table with two large and one small center drawers, pear shaped feet. Walnut cherry, Pennsylvania, 1725-1740.

and, although the imitator may fake the exterior to a darker tone than the interior, he does not make a difference between the colour of the ground at the back of the mounts and that of the surface around them. (The same peculiarity has also been noted on walnut furniture, see page 45).

Concerning the stands, many spurious, elaborately carved and silvered or gilt specimens, similar in design to the examples illustrated, are to be met with. The fine network of cracks over the old gilding already described on page 49, and which on genuine silvered work is, if anything, more pronounced than on the gilt, will not be found on the spurious stands. On examination of the back of a genuine stand it will be seen that the surface of the deal from which the stand is made is left exposed. The imitator, owing to the difficulty of faking these parts on his spurious stand, usually coats them with paint; in fact, he will sometimes silver or gild a spurious stand, and then entirely paint it a dark chocolate-brown or black. Many genuine stands will be found treated in this manner, presumably because a past owner considered a stand too garish or bright in the room and therefore toned down its appearance with paint. Knowing that the collector is aware of the existence of such painted stands, from which it is possible to remove the paint and leave the gilding or silvering underneath intact, the imitator copies such stands and chips and knocks off pieces of the paint, to show to the intending purchaser that he has only to remove the paint to possess a stand with its "original" gilding or silvering.

The carving of the spurious stand has a rounded appearance, and not the crisp, sharp cutting to the foliage and flowers of the genuine example. The design of the foliage with cupids or other *motifs* in the spurious stand will be monotonous and lack the verve of the original. On a genuine stand the gilding in parts, with the composition ground, will have been knocked off, disclosing the deal underneath; these defects will seldom be found on the spurious stand, as if the imitator discloses the new wood of the stand he will have to incur the trouble of making it appear old. A number of genuine cabinets, whose original stands have been lost, or which are plain in character, like those dating from the time of Queen Anne, will have been fictitiously enhanced in value by being mounted on fraudulent stands, generally of an elaborate design, displaying lion heads, or Indian masks. As already mentioned, this later type of gilt stand is to-day exceptionally rare; in fact, much more so than the gilt or silvered example of the seventeenth century. A style of leg which the imitator has frequently used on this type of spurious gilt stand is the one similar to that of the stool, Plate XVII (*a*). Such legs on the spurious stands are usually decorated with scaling.

Another variation between the modern and genuine cabinet is that the mounts of the latter are usually water-gilt. The imitator does not generally go to the expense of this treatment, but leaves his mounts in plain brass and tones them down to give them the appearance of age. Such mounts not being lacquered will go dark by exposure to the atmosphere, like the brass handles on walnut furniture as described on page 50.

Genuine Oriental cabinets decorated with incised or cut lacquer are to-day of extreme rarity and considerable value. As already mentioned, the majority of the genuine examples were made up out of the panels of a coromandel screen ; but few of them are found with panels containing a complete design, showing that they were specially made for the cabinet. Although the genuine incised cabinet formed from a screen is extremely rare, the same cannot be said of those cabinets which have been made from screens within recent years. As these screens are decorated on both sides the imitator, in carrying out this conversion, splits down or saws in two each fold, and the lacquer panels thus obtained he cuts up and fits on to the carcases of the cabinets which he has formed from old material. By cutting up a screen in this manner, the imitator is able to make half a dozen incised lacquer cabinets from one screen ; and the value of the cabinets being far in excess of that of the screen, it pays him well to carry out this deceit. The imitator, besides making these incised cabinets from old screens, also makes many examples with new incised lacquer, of which lacquer it is possible for him to make a passable imitation. In reproducing it, he first covers the surface of the wood with thin successive layers of a preparation of whiting and size, to form the coating in which the design is to be cut. The process of cutting he sometimes simplifies by covering the prepared surface with a thin coating of wax, on which he prints a transfer of the design, and then removes the wax where required by the pattern. Acid is applied on the surface and this eats into the composition ground where it is not protected by the wax, the corrosive action of the acid being stopped when it has proceeded far enough. On removal of the wax the surface will be found etched away according to the design. By this means the cutting out of the design in the composition ground is accomplished with far less expenditure of time and labour than if the work was done by hand.

The difference between old and new incised lacquer is specially noticeable in the colouring, that of the latter being garish and inharmonious compared with the soft and richer colours of the old work. The variation in the tone of the green is specially marked ; that on the genuine example is similar to the green on old *famille verte* porcelain, whereas the modern work has the green much harsher and more blue in tone ; the difference between the reds is also equally pronounced.

When a modern piece of incised lacquer is damaged, it will show the white or grey ground formed by the composition underneath ; but on the genuine incised lacquer the ground, where disclosed, will be of a dark brown colour, resembling papier mâché, as it was chiefly composed of very fine clay, gum and vegetable fibre. The highly polished, hard lacquer which covers the ground on the flat surfaces will, as already mentioned, crack and chip off like veneer. This will not be seen on the imitation.

Bureaux and Bureau-Bookcases

Genuine examples of both these pieces in English lacquer have survived, but there are many more bureau-bookcases than bureaux. Examples of the small bureau-on-legs are also extant ; but rare as the walnut specimens are, the lacquer ones are still rarer.

The bureau-bookcase is found with the black, red and green grounds. A fine example with the green ground is shown in Plate XXXVIII. The green and red, however, are by no means so frequently seen as the black. The narrow bureau-bookcase in lacquer would be a very rare piece to find, and although a number must have been made, very few have survived in comparison with the number of the more ordinary examples of 3 feet to 3 feet 6 inches. Unfortunately, many genuine specimens of the bureau-bookcase, decorated with the English lacquer, will be found in bad condition, especially in regard to the fall-front of the bureau. Notes concerning the mirrors in the walnut bureau-bookcase also refer to those in the lacquer examples.

Spurious imitations of these articles will not be found of new construction like the cabinets, but will be old examples with their surfaces lacquered, bureaux being specially favoured by the imitator for this treatment. To detect these old pieces, with drawers, which have been decorated with modern lacquer, examination should be made of the front of the drawer and the drawer sides, as the imitator often allows the lacquer to flow over the dovetails on the sides, which he forgets to fake like the lacquering on the drawer front. If, therefore, the paint or lacquer on the front edges of the drawer sides has a fresh appearance, suspicion should be aroused.

Oriental examples of these pieces (see Plate XXXIX), are much rarer than those decorated with English lacquer. The Oriental bureau-bookcase will not be found with mirror panels in the top part similar to the English specimen, but will have lacquered panels as in the example illustrated.

Chairs

The surviving lacquer chairs from their design are of the early eighteenth-century type. This tends to show, as already stated, that the seventeenth-

PLATE LV

Dr. George P. Coopernail Collection
Metropolitan Museum of Art
Formerly Francis P. Garvan Collection
Ginsburg & Levy, Inc.

Tables of Queen Anne Period

(Top, left) Large oval table, birch, New England, circa 1735. (Bottom, left) Large oval table, originally in Schuyler mansion, Albany, New York, mahogany, circa 1750. (Top, right) Large table with both leaves raised, walnut, Pennsylvania, circa 1735. (Bottom, right) Smaller six-legged, walnut table, New Jersey or Pennsylvania, circa 1740.

century lacquer pieces were mainly confined to cabinets, and that other articles decorated with it date from the first twenty-five or thirty years of the eighteenth century. Chairs are found both in the English "japan" and the Oriental lacquer, the former being generally of the type with cabriole legs, and a shaped hooped-back and central splat. A type of hall chair with high, solid back and a wooden lacquered seat has survived decorated in Oriental lacquer. Both the English and Oriental lacquer chairs are, however, extremely rare. Undoubtedly, a quantity must have been made, but the small number surviving is attributable to the fact that a chair, of all articles, is one on which the lacquer is most likely to get damaged or worn, and being made of beech they would not be likely to be preserved after the lacquer decoration had become shabby.

The imitator makes lacquer chairs generally of new construction, both because genuine chairs of the period are too rare and valuable to be lacquered, and because, in a chair, only the undersides of the seat-rails are left unlacquered, and these do not give him much trouble to fake, especially if he makes the rails out of old material.

Tables

The lacquer table to-day is extremely rare. A few examples of the oblong tables with scroll legs are extant in the English lacquer; and a few specimens of both the early circular-top card table of the William and Mary period and the later square-top card table with cabriole legs have also survived. Oriental lacquer card tables are not unknown; but the extreme rarity of all types of lacquer tables, and the very bad state of repair of the tops of those that are extant, make the specimen that is in good condition an extremely valuable piece. Specimens of the seventeenth-century oblong table, decorated with incised Oriental lacquer, are also known, but these are of extreme rarity and value.

The commercial imitator makes many card tables of new construction. He also lacquers the plain oak or mahogany tripod-table, and sometimes the oak gate-legged table; but such examples the collector should ignore, as not only are they in bad taste, but they bear no resemblance to any genuine lacquer table of the period.

Chests-with-Drawers and Chests-with-Stands

A number of chests-with-drawers have survived, but, like the rest of the lacquered furniture, these pieces, especially their tops, are seldom found in good repair. The lacquer chest-on-stand, similar to the walnut example, is seldom found with the stand intact; the majority being

PLATE LVI

Israel Sack, Inc.
Formerly Morris Berry
Ginsburg & Levy, Inc.
Ginsburg & Levy, Inc.

Tray-top Tea Tables

(Top, left) Cherry, Connecticut, circa 1740-1750. (Bottom, left) Walnut, Rhode Island, circa 1750. (Top, right) Connecticut, mahogany, circa 1740. (Bottom, right) Possibly by craftsman recently arrived from England. Has ornateness of early Georgian. Mahogany, Pennsylvania, circa 1750-1760.

remounted on modern stands.* These chests-with-drawers and chests-on-stands are nearly always found with a black ground, examples with either red, blue, or green grounds being very exceptional, especially those of the first-named colour.

The chest-with-drawers is a very favourite piece for the imitator to reproduce with his spurious lacquer; and he is particularly fond of the red background, knowing full well the attractiveness that it adds to a piece. He either uses old walnut chests-with-drawers from which he strips off the veneer, or the oak chests-with-drawers; and, occasionally, he will use mahogany chests. Needless to say, if a collector comes across a piece of lacquer furniture, the carcase of which is made of mahogany, he need not carry his investigations any further, as he has obtained sufficient proof of the spurious nature of the example. The favourite type of mahogany chest-with-drawers that the imitator uses for his lacquer work is one without the projecting top, and with the overlapping drawer front, as these chests, which are fairly numerous, are more in consonance with the furniture of the lacquer period. Although he will not be guilty of lacquering a bow-fronted chest-with-drawers, as such chests date from the last quarter of the eighteenth century, he will often forget to pierce his new lacquer on the outsides of the drawer fronts to correspond with the holes of former sets of handles, as described on page 97.

Chests

A number of Oriental chests with domed or flat lids have survived, both in the raised and in the incised lacquer. Such chests were imported from the East in the time of William and Mary and later, and were mounted on English stands, sometimes with turned and tapered legs connected by stretchers, and occasionally with supports of a more elaborate design, such as carved and gilt eagles or dragons. Other specimens are found, especially of the type with the flat lid, with a plain plinth or bracket foot without the stand. The majority of these chests are found in the Oriental lacquer, and not in the English "japan."

A number of spurious examples decorated with incised lacquer have been made by the imitator, usually mounted on gilt stands, of a design with cabriole legs, sometimes elaborately decorated with masks. Many genuine

* To detect a modern stand to an old lacquer chest a comparison should be made of the drawers in the stand with the drawers in the chest. If the stand is genuine, the construction, dovetailing and the wood used for its drawer linings will be identical with those of the chest. In a spurious stand the drawers might be made of pine, with dovetailing of the later type, whereas the drawers of the chest might be of oak with the dovetails extending to the front of the drawer.

PLATE LVII

Ginsburg & Levy, Inc.

Queen Anne Sideboard Table

Walnut frame and marble top. Originally belonged to the Babbitt family of Wickford, Rhode Island. Made about 1725-1750. Above it hangs an American Queen Anne mirror with curved and shaped walnut frame. Philadelphia, circa 1720-1730.

chests have also been mounted on new stands, and the stands, therefore, should always receive careful examination from the collector.

The modern incised lacquer chest has a very different appearance to the genuine example, being nearly always too bright and new looking. The old examples are, unfortunately, too often in bad repair; and, on those with the raised-pattern Oriental lacquer, the colours are very much sunk in, and the gilding is worn away.

Dressing-Tables

A number of pedestal dressing-tables of large size, measuring about 4 feet in width, similar to the example illustrated, Plate XXXVI (*b*), have survived, decorated either in the Oriental or the English "japan" lacquer. The survival of such large examples in lacquer is all the more remarkable in view of the fact that large walnut dressing-tables of this size, as already commented upon, are practically unknown. These large dressing-tables cannot be considered as writing-tables, for they invariably have the decorated top, and not one covered with velvet or leather, as they would undoubtedly have if made for writing purposes.

The smaller pedestal dressing-table, similar to the example illustrated in walnut, Plate XXXIV (*a*), is known in both English and Oriental lacquer; and lacquer examples of the other dressing-table on legs have also survived. All these three types of tables are to-day of great rarity, and although a large number must have been made originally, few have been able to sustain the two centuries of wear and tear.

The Secretaire with Fall-Down Front

This piece in lacquer is not unknown to-day, although the majority of the existing examples are decorated with the English and not the Oriental variety.

As already stated, a number of spurious examples of this piece have been made by the imitator, and a lacquered specimen, therefore, should always be closely examined before an opinion as to its authenticity is arrived at.

Mirrors and Toilet-Glasses

The decoration of the frames of wall mirrors with the English japan must have been much in vogue during the reigns of William and Mary and Queen Anne, as a number have survived. The early mirror, with heavy moulded frame, is not unknown to-day in lacquer; but the majority of existing examples are of the narrow, vertical type, with half-round moulded frame, surmounted by a hood. Unfortunately, many of these mirrors are in bad condition, with the hoods missing, and the frames are often badly worm-eaten. The majority of the lacquer mirrors will be found with the black ground, although examples with a red ground are not unknown, and in other colours they are extremely rare.

The lacquer mirror has received considerable attention from the imitator as he has lacquered many old mirror frames in walnut and mahogany. He has sometimes committed the error of lacquering genuine mirrors, sometimes of mahogany, that are too late in date to be found decorated in this manner. The notes concerning the genuine mirror plate on page 135 also apply to mirrors with lacquer frames.

The toilet glass is another piece to be found decorated with English "japan" lacquer; and unlike the other pieces of lacquered furniture a number of genuine specimens have survived with the rare red ground. Many of these toilet glasses will be found with the mirror and side supports restored, and only the base-with-drawers original. Unfortunately, the majority of existing examples are in poor condition with the lacquer damaged or disfigured.

The imitator has not been behindhand in supplying lacquer toilet-glasses, made from the large quantity of plain mahogany examples surviving. In examining these glasses it should not be forgotten by the collector that a lacquered mahogany example can generally be recognized, if one of the drawers in the base is taken out, as many of these mirrors were made in solid mahogany, and in consequence, the sides will be formed of this wood. The backs of the drawer fronts will usually be of mahogany also.

Corner Cupboards

The tall lacquer corner-cupboard, similar to the walnut examples, invariably has solid and not glazed doors. This piece with the latter doors is of a spurious character, being the late eighteenth-century mahogany or oak corner-cupboard converted into a lacquer specimen.

The hanging corner-cupboard with convex doors and decorated with lacquer has survived in considerable numbers. This was a piece that, like the long-case clock, continued to be made in lacquer in the country districts long after the early eighteenth-century lacquer had gone out of vogue. Such corner-cupboards, unless decorated with red lacquer, or possessing some other interesting feature, are not of great value, to-day, owing to the difficulty of hanging them in a modern room. A number of contemporary Dutch lacquer examples will also be met with in England, but these can be recognized by the coarseness of the lacquer and the poor drawing of the design. A number of spurious examples made by lacquering old oak or mahogany specimens are also to be found.

Long-Case, Bracket, and Wall Clocks

The case of the long-case clock has already been mentioned as a very favourite article to be treated with lacquer decoration. The earliest examples date from the beginning of William and Mary's reign, and these lacquer cases, as previously noted, continued to be made throughout the eighteenth century. Examples of these clock-cases with green and blue lacquer, unlike the other lacquer furniture, are often found; and, like the toilet-glass, a number have survived with the red ground. A few examples have also survived with the rare yellow ground; and these, perhaps, are the only genuine pieces extant with this rare colour.

The bracket clock was another favoured article for decoration with lacquer, and examples with the black and green grounds are not uncommon, and the red lacquer is also fairly common on the cases of these clocks. Bracket clock-cases, unlike the long clock-cases, do not appear to have been made in lacquer later than about 1750.

Lacquer as a decoration for wall clocks was also much in vogue, although it is generally of poor quality compared with the lacquer found on the furniture; and in some cases the decoration consists only of gold lines, without any design of figures or landscapes. These wall clocks are usually found with the black and not the coloured grounds. The least valuable examples are those with circular dials, but rare specimens that are more sought after have octagonal or arched dials.

A very large number of genuine oak or walnut long clock-cases have been converted into lacquer examples by the imitator; in fact, he has lacquered so many plain cases within recent years that the genuine lacquer examples form but a small fraction of the lacquered cases in existence.

The black, pearwood-case bracket clock is also a very favourite piece for this treatment, as owing to its black case, it is not a very saleable type; and the imitator has been able, therefore, to buy examples at a low price for conversion into lacquer specimens.

CHAPTER VIII

FURNITURE AS AMERICANS PREFERRED IT

BETWEEN English and American furniture there has always been a well-defined half-brother relationship. When pieces of the same period are seen separately, a strong family resemblance is evident; but when they are placed side by side, this fades.

In Part I the reader has spent a week end, so to speak, with the English Age of Walnut. During it he has met the good-looking and fashionably turned out members of this inanimate family circle. Also, Mr. Symonds has been at hand briefing him on the merits and distinctive points of the walnut group. In Part II we come to America, where we shall follow the fortunes of the robust half-brothers, all younger by a quarter of a century or more, and we shall see many things happen that would not have been considered cricket at the ancestral manor.

Both English walnut furniture and American furniture of corresponding styles had their own characteristics and reflected specific social settings. Imagine the time as January 1, 1700. The place is the green room in the substantial home of Puritan Judge Samuel Sewall, near Boston Common. Seated at a kneehole writing table of crotch-grained veneer, which is beautified with elaborate marquetry (see Plate XIV), Judge Sewall moves his pen methodically over a page in his diary: "Just about Break-a Day Jacob Amsden and 3 other trumpeters gave a Blast on the common near Mr. Alford's—entrance of the 18th Century—The Trumpeters cost me five pieces $\frac{8}{8}$."

It is June 12, 1712, in London, and in White's Chocolate House "Dick" Steele, seated in a banister-back chair of curly maple (see Plate XLIV), is bending over a butterfly table painted red (see Plate LIII). He, too, is writing; his subject is "Dueling." He is doing his stint for the *Spectator*, famous weekly of comment on manners and events, and model for scores of others thereafter, including *Punch* and our present-day *New Yorker*.

Both of these events are recorded happenings, but there is something wrong with each picture. The furniture needs shifting. In the Boston of 1700, an ornate kneehole table, then the height of London fashion, would have been unthinkable in the house of a man who frowned on personal adornment as foolish and sinful. "Having heard last night that Josiah Willard had cut off his hair (a very full head of hair) and put on a Wigg, I went to him this morning," he writes in his diary for

PLATE LVIII

Gallery of Fine Arts, Yale University
Metropolitan Museum of Art
Formerly Blin W. Page Collection
Dr. George P. Coopernail Collection

William and Mary Chests of Drawers

(Top, left) A New England type. Curly maple with ball feet, circa 1700-1710. (Bottom, left) Painted with Chinese motifs to approximate Oriental lacquer. Connecticut, circa 1700-1710. (Top, right) Small chest of drawers with burl walnut veneered drawer fronts. Top and feet of pine, circa 1700. (Bottom, right) Six drawer-high chest of drawers, curly maple, ball feet, originally painted black, Connecticut, circa 1690-1710.

1701. "Prayed him to read the Tenth Chapter of the Third book of Calvin's Institutions." Fifty years later a modified form of the kneehole writing table (see Plate LX), complete with central cupboard in the base for a "Wigg," would appear as a Queen Anne survival piece. It would reflect a less austere social outlook, but still be less ornate than English furniture of the same period.

Equally out of place in London would have been the butterfly table and the banister-back chair. These were brought to a high point of beauty in America, fine enough for people of the top-income brackets, but in England they remained unadorned provincial pieces for country gentry and the like.

The English Age of Walnut was approximately from 1660 to 1730, a span of about seventy years; in the American colonies its equivalent covered the years between 1670 and 1750, with some thirty years more added when characteristically American pieces of furniture, notably the block-fronts of Rhode Island, were made in a design basically Queen Anne.

Since current events and prevailing social and economic conditions are always determining factors in household furnishing, especially in furniture, a brief look at the American colonies in the mid-seventeenth and early eighteenth centuries might be profitable. Although the English had been making a consistent business of establishing colonies along the Atlantic seaboard since 1607, progress had been anything but streamlined. It took really venturesome men and women to risk a voyage of six to eight weeks which landed them on an untamed shore, inhabited by Indians and wild beasts. There were three tries before Virginia was really under way; and only the vigorous opposition of their religious views at home sent Pilgrims and Puritans to New England.

By 1660, when Charles II and his court brought over a new style of furniture from France and the Low Countries, where they had spent their years of exile, the American colonies numbered only six—Massachusetts, Rhode Island, Connecticut and New Hampshire in the north; Virginia and Maryland in the south. Four years later territory in between, held by the Dutch, was surrendered to England and the colonies of New York, New Jersey and Delaware emerged, the latter not being fully organized until 1691. Pennsylvania, later to become one of the chief cabinetmaking areas, was still virgin forest, and in the Carolinas settlement had barely begun. Along this thin coastal fringe there were possibly a hundred thousand colonists, with a large proportion located in New England.

It is easy to see why the new-style walnut furniture took thirty years to be accepted in America. Before 1690, the colonists were more concerned with pushing inland and expanding than in acquiring the latest London furniture styles. Moreover, in New England, where the majority of cabinetmakers were located, there was little love for the Stuart monarchs, and James II did nothing to ease the situation. Both he and his older brother Charles considered the American colonies as much their personal possession as Hampton Court or Windsor Castle.

PLATE LIX

Ginsburg & Levy, Inc.
Anonymous
Dr. George P. Coopernail Collection
Ginsburg & Levy, Inc.

Queen Anne Chests of Drawers

(Top, left) Chest of drawers on frame, maple, Massachusetts, circa 1720-1740. (Bottom, left) Six drawer high chest of age-darkened curly maple. New York or New Jersey, circa 1750-1760. (Top, right) Four drawer chest, cherry, Connecticut, circa 1740-1750. (Bottom, right) Chest-on-frame. Has valanced skirt and cabriole legs, New Hampshire, circa 1740-1760.

In 1685, when a stroke of apoplexy ended the reign of Charles II, the new king started almost at once to carry out the colonial measures his brother had had in mind. The first step was to appoint Sir Edmund Andros governor of Massachusetts. A dull, dogged army officer determined to carry out orders, he began by abolishing local colonial government. He decreed the General Court of Massachusetts out of existence and transferred all government authority to himself and his council. Two years later, Connecticut and Rhode Island were placed under his administration and their charters revoked. Boston became the sole seat of government, and arbitrary tax schedules were promulgated. New York was next put under the proconsulship of Andros, who ruled like a dictator. Taxes were as he decreed them; a press censorship was established; common lands were seized; and the writ of habeas corpus, practically the foundation stone of English justice, was suspended. New England colonists were informed that only by their paying high quit rents or fees would Governor Andros give royal confirmation to the land owned under the abolished colonial charters.

At the trial of the Reverend John Wise of Ipswich, who had publicly challenged Andros' dictatorial acts, the Crown contended that Americans had no rights save that of not being sold as slaves. New England was in a ferment, as were all liberty-loving Englishmen, both at home and in America. On April 4, 1689, John Winslow brought word that James II had fled and William, Prince of Orange, had landed in England to receive the crown for himself and his wife Mary. Two weeks later Andros was taken prisoner, and under the new monarchs Massachusetts received a new royal charter; those of Connecticut and Rhode Island were restored; and in time separate royal governors arrived with liberal instructions and self-government was again in force.

Naturally, William and Mary were popular with the American colonists; and, logically, things British, including furniture, were looked upon with favor. Gradually New England and the other colonies came out of the depression that Stuart misrule had brought about, and many orders came to the cabinetmakers for new furniture. Thus we can understand today why the date "*circa* 1690" is given so frequently for certain American furniture. And the fact that the co-monarchs undid the arbitrary actions that Charles II had contemplated and his brother had sent Andros to accomplish, may explain why so much American furniture was made in the William and Mary style and so little in the Stuart. Also, there was no thirty years' lag between the William and Mary and the Queen Anne periods. Indeed, the change from one to the other was no more deliberate than would be expected in a day of slow communication.

By the time Queen Anne designs began to filter through, about 1710, all but one of the thirteen colonies were well established and prosperous. America was experiencing the first stirrings of style consciousness and was looking to England for new furniture ideas.

CHAPTER IX

CABINETWOODS USED IN AMERICA

IF WE go back to the beginning of the Age of Walnut in England, we find that the Stuart style marked a drastic change in furniture construction and cabinetwood. During the early years of the seventeenth century, when the first colonists were emigrating to America, massive architectural chests, tables, chairs and cupboards of oak formed the chief furnishings of English homes. With the Restoration came a new design from the Low Countries and a different cabinetwood, common on the Continent, thanks to the Romans, who had originally introduced the Persian walnut into Italy. There it had thrived, and gradually spread to other parts of Europe.

Walnut trees from across the Channel had also been planted in England a century before to take the place of the many oaks that had been cut in the woodlands and hunting parks in the course of building the British fleet that defended England against the Spanish Armada. These trees, so thriftily planted in Queen Elizabeth's reign, now furnished cabinetwood for the craftsmen who were soon busy adapting the new style to the tastes of their clients.

As already stated, Americans clung to their wainscot and oak house furnishings for years after they had been outmoded in England, shifting gradually and reluctantly to the Stuart style and then with increasing enthusiasm to the William and Mary and the Queen Anne. But when colonial craftsmen finally convinced their clients that the age of oak was over, they, too, looked in their own back yards for cabinetwood and found plenty of walnut, as well as eight or ten varieties of native hardwoods well suited to furniture making. They included maple, birch, cherry, ash, butternut and hickory. Of these, hard maple and black and yellow birch were new cabinetwoods, since such trees did not grow either in England or on the Continent.

In New England, which had more cabinetmakers at the time than all the other colonies combined, maple and birch grew in the primeval forests, and they often occurred in fancy grains. The decorative value of curly and bird's-eye maple and curly birch was duly appreciated by cabinetmakers and these woods were widely used. Much fine furniture was made of them in the Stuart, William and Mary and Queen Anne styles, for which only walnut was used in England. In fact, study of sales catalogues of principal collections of American antique furniture

PLATE LX

Gallery of Fine Arts, Yale University
Formerly James Curran
Ginsburg & Levy, Inc.

William and Mary Desks

(Top, center) Slant-top desk. Lid and drawer fronts of burl walnut veneer, ball feet, painted black, New England, 1700-1720. (Bottom, left) Desk-on-frame. Design similar to lowboys of same style. Walnut, Philadelphia, circa 1700. (Lower right) New Jersey applewood desk inlaid and dated. Top drawer bears initials of John Craddock, original owner. Lid inlaid with song birds, other drawers with stars. Date, 1760.

sold since the famous Reifsnyder Collection in 1929 shows that the proportion of furniture made by colonial craftsmen during these years was probably four pieces in other hardwoods to one of walnut.

However, walnut also grew in the forests, the largest stands of it being in Pennsylvania and Virginia, and it was by no means slighted by American craftsmen. It was of a different variety from that of England. The popular name for it, black walnut, had nothing to do with the tone of the wood, but was descriptive of the color of the shells of its nuts. The wood varied in color, according to the region in which the trees grew. In New England, it was brown; in New York and New Jersey, it took on a reddish tinge; and it became distinctly "red Virginia walnut" in southern Pennsylvania, Delaware, Maryland and Virginia.

The black tone of American walnut in the nineteenth century was the result of deliberate tinting before varnishing. This treatment, which "killed" its natural reddish tone, was never used by eighteenth-century cabinetmakers. As the best native walnut came from trees growing inland from about Philadelphia to North Carolina, it was a common practice for New England coastal ships to include walnut plank in their cargoes when they sailed homeward from southern ports. Peter Faneuil of Boston on a number of occasions gave masters of his ships specific instructions to bring home walnut lumber "fit for cabinetmakers' use."

Job Townsend and his son-in-law, John Goddard, of Newport, Rhode Island, made much of their Queen Anne furniture, including some block-front pieces, of this Virginia red walnut. In the first half of the eighteenth century Newport was no summer play spot, but was headquarters for whaling, privateering and slave trading. The same schooners, snows and ketches that took away newly arrived Africans to be converted into plantation field hands, brought in planks of desirable Virginia walnut. In addition, there were many small sailing ships, mostly owned by amphibious New Englanders engaged in the coastal and West Indian trade. These boats were of shallow draft; and practically any cove, inlet or river mouth was deep enough for one of them to come to port with a cargo that could be unloaded without encountering royal or colonial inspectors. Merchants knew full well the extra profits a cruise would yield if port fees and the like could be avoided, and they took advantage of such bootlegging whenever possible. So, by legal and illegal means, red walnut found its way into the shops of New England cabinetmakers.

Another well-regarded hardwood was cherry. There were several varieties, but that most used for furniture was the black or wild cherry, found widely scattered through the forests—a small clump here, another there, but never large stands at any one place. This wood had a fine grain, sometimes curly. Furniture made of it took on a rich red-brown color when finished that was slightly lighter in tone than that of the best walnut.

There was also the wood of the butternut tree, much like walnut but lighter

PLATE LXI

Formerly Harold S. Hanks Collection
Ginsburg & Levy, Inc.
Ginsburg & Levy, Inc.
Dr. George P. Coopernail Collection

Queen Anne Desks

(Top, left) Small desk-on-frame, maple and pine, New England, circa 1750. Above it shelf clock, Queen Anne case, Simon Willard, circa 1770. (Bottom, left) Walnut desk, Pennsylvania, circa 1720-1730. (Right top) Maple desk, New England, 1720-1740. (Right bottom) Maple desk made in 1708 for a Dr. Welch of Connecticut.

in color, so that it was sometimes called white walnut. Some furniture was made of it, and also of ash, hickory and similar native woods. None of these was extensively used for an entire piece but rather for special parts, such as spindles, stretchers and slats.

Because of difficult farming conditions, New England colonists early turned to home manufactures, deep-sea fishing and commerce as more profitable ways to earn a living, and only farmed enough to supply their own needs. It was therefore logical that there should be a good proportion of cabinetmakers in the population, especially by the beginning of the eighteenth century. By that time, most of these were native-born, and in some instances they were third generation. Consequently they had their own American ideas which they incorporated into what they made, giving their furniture an individuality that differentiated it from contemporary English pieces. This was also true of the active, if less numerous, cabinetmakers located in New York, New Jersey, Pennsylvania and Delaware, and occasionally in the more agricultural colonies of Maryland, Virginia, North Carolina and South Carolina.

When these furniture craftsmen, working from New England to South Carolina, forsook oak and wainscot construction for other native hardwoods and the Stuart style, they produced American versions of the new designs rather than copies. Nor did the entire range of English furniture interest them equally. Of some pieces they made only a few; others, not overly popular in England, they developed and made fashionable here. Banister and slat-back chairs and the butterfly table are outstanding examples of furniture that originated in provincial England and was later brought to America and developed into fine pieces for houses of sophisticated people. In fact, this independence of thought with both material and design was a chief characteristic of American craftsmanship during the nearly two centuries of its existence.

CHAPTER X

CHAIRS, DAYBEDS AND SETTEES

AS THE seventeenth century reached its close, American joiners and cabinetmakers began to make chairs that were different in construction and in the idea of their use. Throughout the Puritan period, they had produced the impressive wainscot chair which was almost a seat of state, and turned ones, mostly of the Carver-Brewster type. These were for important personages. Ordinary folk sat on backless joined stools.

The first of the new chairs was the Cromwellian (see Plate XLI) and was called the farthingale in England because it was of a type in which a woman wearing a large hooped petticoat could sit. A very simple chair, it consisted of a framework of two short front legs, two back uprights which were connected by plain and turned stretchers, the latter done with ball-and-bobbin turnings. The seat and low back were covered with either leather or turkey work, which took its name from a similarity to the oriental rug then called a "Turkey carpet." Through a backing of heavy canvas or sacking, wool yarns of various colors, always including red, were looped, in much the way a hooked rug is made. When the work was finished, the yarn was sheared, and the result was a strong upholstery fabric which could be used in place of the more expensive needlepoint then made in England and on the Continent.

Added decoration was sometimes achieved by the use of large brass-headed nails. Such a chair was little more than a joined stool plus a short, uncomfortable back.

From the few examples that have survived, it is probable that not many were made in America. Today even the best museums consider themselves fortunate if, like the Metropolitan Museum of Art, they have one example (see Plate XXXI) in original condition. Of the few so far found, some are of walnut, others of maple or cherry, and a few of oak. In England, these chairs were sometimes made with backs of two carved cross members instead of upholstery, and front legs and cross stretchers were turned in a spiral design, a refinement omitted from those made in America.

About 1700 Americans began to make elaborate high-back chairs with caned seat and back (see Plate XLII) which were copied directly from similar chairs of the Restoration period, the fashion for which had reached England with the re-

PLATE LXII

Richard Loeb Collection

Desk with Sixteen Secret Compartments

A Queen Anne curly maple desk made in New England about 1740, slant-top with simple bracket feet. Note detail of pigeon holes, document and other small drawers. (Below) Some of secret compartments opened to show location.

turn of Charles II. But where the English chairs were universally of walnut and frequently very ornate with their elaborately carved backs, front legs and stretcher, those of colonial America had more turning and practically no carving except on the cresting of the back and on the front stretcher.

One wonders if this was the type of chair in which Judge Sewall sat while pursuing his unsuccessful courtship of the wealthy Widow Winthrop. "I went to Mad. Winthrop; found her rocking her little Katee in the Cradle," he wrote gloomily later. "She set me an arm'd Chair with Cusheon; and so the Cradle was between her arm'd Chair and mine." Even at the turn of the eighteenth century armchairs were not a commonplace in the average household, and so an "arm'd Chair with Cusheon" was obviously a mark of respect, though not always of affection.

Judging by the examples that have survived, the American version of the Restoration chair occasionally had carving on the front stretcher and on the uprights framing the caning of the back. Otherwise, turnings prevailed. Vase, baluster and urn shapes were the motifs used for front and back legs, with the single front stretchers done in bold ball-and-ring turnings. The arms were simple downward cyma curves flaring slightly outward. Two prime examples, the John Hancock armchair and the Sir William Pepperell side chair, are well known to collectors (see Plate XLIII). The Hancock chair is of maple; the Pepperell one of ash and other native hardwoods, and painted a dark color.

Following closely, if not contemporaneously, were two English provincial types which became elaborate enough under the hands of American craftsmen for the homes of wealthy colonists. Both originated in the northern counties and the Midlands, whence had come many of the early American colonists. These chairs were the splat-back (see Plate XLV) and the banister-back (see Plate XLIV), which was a direct off-shoot of the Stuart chair. In the banister-back, four or five split banister turnings replaced the cane-work back, and the seat was of rush. The back had a well-carved top member, or cresting; the front and rear legs were turned in a combination of ball, vase, urn and block turnings. Earlier examples had simply turned front; with later ones the Spanish foot was used. With some, the back was somewhat canted backward. Most of them, however, had a perpendicular back, resulting in a decorative but not too comfortable chair. The idea of a comfortable chair had not yet occurred to either maker or purchaser.

These banister-backs were made both with and without arms. From this chair form it was a ready step to one in which a vase-shaped splat replaced the banisters, and the back cresting became yoke-shaped. Some reflected the coming Queen Anne style in tapered turnings of front legs and simple button feet. A few banister- and splat-back chairs were made in walnut, but many more were produced in maple, cherry and less important hardwoods. Curly maple was a favorite material since its grain was especially decorative for turned parts, back splats and shaped arms.

PLATE LXIII

Metropolitan Museum of Art
Henry F. duPont Collection
Formerly Luke Vincent Lockwood Collection
Ginsburg & Levy, Inc.

From Chest-on-Frame to Highboy

(Top, left) Oak, maple and pine chest-on-frame. New England, 1680-1700. (Bottom, left) Small Chest on stand. Gumwood, made in Dutchess County, New York, circa 1700. (Top, right) William and Mary Highboy. Low base has single wide drawer, short Flemish scroll legs. Cherry, Connecticut, circa 1710. (Right, bottom) Typical American William and Mary highboy. Curly maple, Pennsylvania, circa 1700.

For simpler country chairs at this time, the slat-back was more in favor. An infinite variety, from very plain ones with two or three slats to handsome chairs having up to seven or eight arch-shaped slats, were made in both arm and side chairs. In all of these, the front and rear uprights were turned, simply or elaborately, according to the skill of the craftsman or the taste of his client. Sometimes the front stretcher was very ornamental, being turned with bold ring-and-ball motifs. The slat-back was, of course, an almost basic chair form, and had been evolved from chairs of the Carver-Brewster type. Rarely does one find an example made of walnut. Most of them consisted of a variety of American hardwoods—maple for the uprights, oak or ash for slats and hickory or ash for the stretchers. The slat-back, in fact, continued almost unchanged in style until well into the nineteenth century.

Space-saving, strong and comfortable, the roundabout or corner chair was first cousin to the slat-back. Whether the first American roundabout was imported or was a memory piece, fashioned by a local chairmaker for some client who wanted a comfortable armchair, is not known, but both country and town craftsmen made it from about 1700 through the entire period under consideration, and even later. From the many examples still to be found today, it is apparent that roundabouts fall into two classes—the turned kind, which plainly shows its relationship to the slat-back; and the urban corner chair with cabriole legs and ornamental back splats (see Plate XLVII). Designed to fit into the corner of a room, each type put its best foot forward, with most of the decorative detail concentrated on the front leg. The turned corner chairs were not much influenced by changing fashions. Their ornamentation was achieved by turnings of legs and stretchers, by shaping of arms and back, all according to the taste and skill of the chairmaker. A combination of woods, including hickory, ash and oak, was frequently used in their making.

Urban roundabouts of the Queen Anne period were made by cabinetmakers rather than wood turners. In these, one or all of the legs were cabriole-shaped and terminated in pad feet. Made of walnut, maple, cherry or birch, they were handsome chairs, essentially masculine and high in favor with the head of the house.

About 1715, American cabinetmakers began to produce a handsome chair with upholstered slip seat (see Plate XLVI). Made in the style of Queen Anne, it had well-executed front cabriole legs terminating in pad feet, and the square back uprights were frequently molded on the front surface. The top cresting was either yoke- or hoop-shaped, with central back splat vase-shaped and sometimes pierced. In time, the shape of the seat developed from square to one which flared outward, and finally it took on rounded corners and a curving front, somewhat like the cross section of a bell. Many of these chairs were made with arms nicely executed in cyma curves and terminating in Flemish scrolls. Later examples had well-carved shells on the knees of the front cabriole legs and at the center of the cresting.

By 1725, Americans were demanding a truly comfortable armchair, and to

PLATE LXIV

Metropolitan Museum of Art
Ginsburg & Levy, Inc.
Ginsburg & Levy, Inc.

Representative William and Mary Highboys

(Top, center) Highboy of maple and pine. Japanned to simulate Chinese lacquer. New England, circa 1700. (Bottom, left) Highboy with burl veneer on drawer fronts. Walnut, New England, 1700-1710 (Bottom right) Walnut highboy, six trumpet legs and large ball feet. Pennsylvania, 1700-1710.

meet this the wing chair made its appearance (see Plate XLVIII). The frame was, of course, upholstered and the back was flanked by two wings which protected the occupant from drafts. Such chairs had short front cabriole legs with pad feet and square rear ones, canted backward. A set of three stretchers, either shaped or gracefully turned, connected them. Walnut was most frequently used for the exposed parts, though maple or cherry were also favored. The wing chair saw a great development in America as in England, and culminated in the very handsome chairs of the Philadelphia Chippendale period.

If we can judge by the examples extant, the American daybed (see Plate XLIX) was a most impressive piece of furniture, which saw its high point in ornamentation during the Stuart years. It was then that elaborately carved pieces were made, to be followed in the William and Mary and the Queen Anne periods by well-executed but less embellished ones. In the first of them, made as early as 1690, there was the same use of Flemish curves in the carving and of cane for seat and backrest as was employed in the high-back chairs. These carved daybeds were made of walnut and maple. Later ones were characterized by boldly turned legs and stretchers and a back constructed of a yoke cresting with one broad or three narrow vase splats. In such chairs the earlier cane work was replaced by heavy linen drawn tightly to the frame, on which upholstered pads were placed. Walnut, cherry and plain and curly maple were the woods used.

Use of the cabriole leg marked the Queen Anne style in this piece, a notable example being the daybed made by Job Townsend in 1743 for a prominent Newport family. This daybed, now in the American Wing Collection of the Metropolitan Museum, is made of well-figured curly maple and has six cabriole legs terminating in fairly large pad feet. The legs are braced both lengthwise and crosswise by seven baluster-turned stretchers. The back, which is adjustable, has a central vase-shaped splat supported by two slightly curved posts that extend into a pair of square legs, canted backward. It measures five feet seven inches long and twenty-three inches wide, obviously not being intended for a man of George Washington's proportions.

Although English cabinetmakers produced many handsome settees during the Stuart years and subsequent periods, only a few were made in America, and those few were in the Queen Anne manner. Always sophisticated, expensive pieces, made for the homes of merchant princes, wealthy planters and the like, they were walnut and of the double-chair variety (see Plate L). Later a few other settees were made which were more nearly related to the wing chair, since seat, arms and back were entirely upholstered and the supporting legs and connecting stretchers were the only wood exposed. From the few examples that turn up here and there today, it is logical to infer that these settees were mostly made by cabinetmakers "lately come from London" rather than by native craftsmen whose training and traditions were entirely of the colonies, since study of individual pieces shows fine points of construction and ornamentation that were more frequently English than American.

CHAPTER XI

TABLES OF VARIOUS SORTS

AMERICAN cabinetmakers produced very few large tables during the years immediately following the Puritan period, and those few probably served an ecclesiastical purpose more often than not. They had oblong tops of the refrectory type but were not more than half as long as those of the seventeenth century; the base consisted of four legs and column, braced by four square stretchers placed just above the large ball feet. The earliest small tables had plain oblong tops supported by a framework of ball-turned legs and stretchers. The lower edge of the apron was scalloped and the stretchers on the long side were raised halfway from the floor (see Plate XLI). Usually made with a maple base and a pine top, they were direct copies of the Stuart tables, except for the fact that the turnings were not spiral.

Among their contemporaries was the gateleg table (see Plate LII), which continued in favor as late as 1750. It ranged in size from one having a top not over thirty-six inches wide with leaves raised, to an oval measuring four feet nine inches wide, by five feet eight inches long. A few tables of very large size had double gates, but single ones were usual. All had understructures of square and turned members in which vase, urn, ball and ring turnings provided the ornamentation. Their simple knob feet were often among the casualties of normal wear and tear—so much so that rarely is an antique gateleg found with feet intact. Usually they are either completely worn off or much restored.

Whereas in England the small gatelegs were always of walnut, with walnut underbody and oak top for those of larger size, gatelegs of American craftsmanship were executed in a variety of native woods, such as maple, cherry, birch, ash and walnut. Some combined two or three kinds of wood. They were usually painted dark red or green.

Some years ago, in Vermont, I saw a most unusual gateleg. Of medium size, it had a curly maple top, and legs and stretchers of pear wood executed in bold ball-and-urn turnings. Of Rhode Island origin, it had been brought to northern New England by a grandson of the original owner, a full century after it was made. Because of the small size of the tree, pear wood could, of course, be used only for turned parts, but this blended with the curly maple top so that the entire effect was that of a glowing rich honey tone.

PLATE LXV

Metropolitan Museum of Art
Ginsburg & Levy, Inc.
Museum of Fine Arts, Boston

Typical Queen Anne Highboys

(Top, center) Bonnet top highboy. Gilded finials and carved shell. Japanned to imitate Chinese lacquer. Maple and pine. Boston, circa 1735. (Bottom, left) Burl walnut veneer front, curly maple sides. Cornice molding conceals secret drawer. New England, 1720-1730. (Bottom, right) Curly maple highboy, fan carved on central drawer of base. Connecticut, 1735-1750.

A very interesting form of folding table was the small gateleg known as a "tuckaway," so-called because of its narrow bed and wide drop leaves. It had two instead of four legs, a pair of block feet about six inches long, and a single central stretcher, on which the two gates hinged.

About 1725, some fine examples of a table of the gateleg variety were made in walnut. The legs, which terminated in Spanish feet, and the stretchers were especially delicate and turned in a column shape. Very light in construction, this variety of table has long been known as a "spider" table, though the makers of it probably had no such creature in mind at the time they fashioned it. In fact, practically all of the descriptive terms now applied to various pieces of furniture are latter-day appellations of the past fifty years.

The so-called butterfly table (see Plate LIII) was a direct outgrowth of the gateleg and was principally made in Connecticut. It acquired its name in recent years from the two winglike brackets that support the leaves of the top. This table, with its underbody of baluster-turned legs and square stretchers, was long regarded as entirely a product of America, but within the last few years proof has appeared that tables of this sort were made in oak and beech in provincial England during the Restoration. It is clear, therefore, that the butterfly was really a furniture form brought from the British homeland and developed in southern New England into an important piece of colonial furniture.

Made from late in the seventeenth century to about 1740, these tables were made mostly of maple, and occasionally of cherry, sometimes with pine top. Rarely was walnut used. Those of plain-grained wood were usually painted red, green, or blue. The top was square, oblong or oval, rarely round. This type of table was made only in southern New England, and the demand for it seems not to have extended beyond that area. When new, it was probably an occasional table designed for use in the best rooms of simple houses. Surviving examples are small, being from two to four inches lower than gateleg tables of the same period.

With the Queen Anne style thoroughly established in the colonies, a great variety of drop-leaf tables were made with graceful cabriole legs, ending in pad or web feet (see Plate LV). Most of them had four legs, but some of the larger tables were equipped with two extra ones which swung out and supported the wide leaves. In size, these tables varied from the very small, which were hardly large enough for use as a tea table, to large pieces which could accommodate eight to twelve people. They were made in walnut, cherry, maple, applewood and occasionally the lesser hardwoods. Their popularity continued until about 1760, and they held their own even against the newer style of Chippendale with its decorative carving and claw-and-ball foot, which were the marks of the newest in furniture thought.

A very graceful piece during these years was the oblong tea table without leaves. In this the top was framed by a raised molding which gave it the form of a

PLATE LXVI

Ginsburg & Levy, Inc.
Anonymous
Formerly William Randolph Hearst Collection

Three American Chests-on-chests

(Left) Bonnet top, cherry, Hartford, Connecticut, 1760-1770. (Center) Block-front base and low bonnet top with flame finials. Mahogany, Massachusetts, 1765-1770. (Right) Architectural motifs of William Kent's designs reflected in this mahogany piece. Salem, Massachusetts, late eighteenth century.

tray (see Plate LVI) and served as a safeguard for the fine porcelain teasets imported from England and the Orient in the early years of the eighteenth century, when tea drinking first became an established custom in the colonies. Made of either walnut or cherry, tables of this sort were intended for handsome homes in the larger centers.

For sturdy use throughout the American colonies, another type of table, also without leaves, was widely made, especially in New York, New Jersey and Pennsylvania. Known as a tavern table (see Plate LIV), it had four turned legs of baluster form, connected by plain stretchers and terminating in ample ball feet. More frequently than not, from one to three drawers were built into the underbody. These tables were made from about 1690 to 1750 and were little affected by changing styles. They ranged in size from four to seven feet in length and from thirty to thirty-six inches in width. Many of them, especially in Pennsylvania, were entirely of walnut; others were of maple, cherry or birch. Some, particularly the larger ones, had soft-wood tops consisting either of a single board or of two boards adroitly joined. Similar tables were made throughout England for use in the homes of the less affluent, and also in taverns, hence the name.

CHAPTER XII

PIECES ON FRAME AND OTHERS

WITH all of the "case" pieces—that is, those which are enclosed and have drawers—the use of a framework with turned uprights and connecting stretchers instead of feet was characteristic of furniture construction, both in England and America, from the Stuart through the Queen Anne years. It is with such pieces that one sees the desk evolve from a writing box; the chest of drawers from a plain chest; and the highboy from a chest or cabinet with a single drawer beneath. The very earliest of the frames in America had spiral-turned uprights, but more of them were ornamented with ball-and-urn turnings.

About 1725, the Queen Anne influence replaced the turned uprights with cabriole legs, and a decorative apron with lower edge cut in balancing cyma curves enhanced the framework. This use of the frame should be borne in mind when considering the development of all these pieces of furniture, because it was a characteristic of all of them, save the William and Mary chests of drawers and slant-top desks which were supported by large ball feet.

The chest of drawers was a logical development of the six-board chest into which a single wide drawer, or two parallel narrower ones, had been inserted at the bottom. By 1680 American cabinetmakers had begun to produce a chest of drawers which rested on a frame base. This was followed shortly by a typical William and Mary piece with ball feet replacing the frame (see Plate LVIII).

Then in the Queen Anne period the frame returned, having sprouted four cabriole legs with pad feet, and a highly decorative shaped apron. On it rested a tall chest of drawers with six drawers of decreasing size placed one above the other (see Plate LIX). Made of such woods as walnut, maple, plain and fancy-grained, cherry and applewood, they were in favor throughout the colonies from Maine to Maryland.

In the walnut pieces of the William and Mary style, crotch and oyster veneer was sometimes used for the drawer fronts. Veneer was not used in the Queen Anne period and seldom was inlay employed. When it did appear, it was generally for wedding furniture, in which the bride's initials and the date were inlaid in a lighter wood. Chests of this type, with simple bracket feet instead of a frame, were made as late as the last decade of the eighteenth century.

PLATE LXVII

Formerly Richard H. Dana Collection
Museum of Fine Arts, Boston
Metropolitan Museum of Art

Three Handsome Block-front Secretaries

(Left) Reeded pilasters flank doors of upper part. Once owned by Richard H. Dana, author of *Two Years Before the Mast.* Mahogany, circa 1770. (Center) Secretary with arched doors, short cabriole legs. Mahogany, Massachusetts, 1765-1770. (Right) Made by John Goddard of Newport, Rhode Island. Open to show details of interior. Design more Queen Anne than Chippendale. Mahogany, 1760-1775.

The late George Horace Lorimer had in his collection a fine example in which the fronts of the three small drawers at the top had the initials D. H. and the date, 1793, inlaid in holly. The piece was of rich Pennsylvania walnut. This was, of course, a survival piece, made in the Queen Anne manner by a rural Pennsylvania Dutch cabinetmaker, over a half century after the style had passed out of fashion.

The earliest desk was in reality a writing box resting on a frame similar to that of the joined stool, but taller. Such desks were in two parts, and at first the writing was done on the upper side of the lid. Then the sloping lid was hinged at the bottom and the interior provided with pigeonholes and small drawers. Later a large drawer was added in the base, and gradually desks of this type were made all in one piece, though the two-piece shaping was retained.

In the William and Mary period, American cabinetmakers also made slant-top desks with several drawers below and with large ball feet instead of a supporting frame (see Plate LX). Practically all such desks were of walnut, and many of them had fine crotch or burl veneer panels on lid and drawer fronts. When this was done, banding was also used, but the ornate marquetry found on similar English pieces was not attempted. The same held true for the comparatively few William and Mary large fall-front desks made in the colonies at the start of the eighteenth century. These were in two parts. The front of the upper one was hinged at the bottom and when open served as the writing surface. In the base, which stood on large ball feet, were three full-width drawers of graduating depth. This was a desk of Dutch origin. When made in England it was frequently a most ornate piece by reason of elaborate inlay and marquetry done in contrasting colors to the walnut veneer with which the carcass was faced.

With the Queen Anne period, Americans returned to the use of a supporting frame (see Plate LXI) which took the form of cabriole legs, terminating in pad feet, and an ornamental apron which sometimes contained a single wide drawer. Later examples were made with several drawers beneath the writing flap, when the bases of such pieces had much shorter cabriole legs, but the apron was still cut in pleasing curves.

Later, after use of the frame had ceased, Queen Anne desks were made with very short cabriole legs and pad feet, as well as with plain and molded bracket feet. Walnut, maple, plain and fancy, cherry, birch and a combination of hardwoods were used for these slant-top desks with four graduated drawers. Such desks were so popular that they continued to be made in the more remote sections even as late as the Hepplewhite and Sheraton years. They were uncarved and without inlay ornamentation; their beauty lay in good lines, nice proportion and fine-grained wood. Many of them, especially those originating south of Connecticut, were made of walnut of such a rich red tint that at first glance the wood could be mistaken for mahogany.

PLATE LXVIII

Formerly Francis P. Garvan Collection
Israel Sack, Inc.

William and Mary Lowboys

(Top) Shallow central drawer in bed, flanked by deeper ones. Trumpet legs braced by transverse stretchers. New England, 1700-1720. (Bottom) Curly maple in original finish, top natural, base stained to simulate walnut, delicately turned trumpet legs. New Jersey or Pennsylvania, 1700-1710.

In New England, particularly in Rhode Island and Massachusetts, cabinetmakers used the best grade of Virginia red walnut for their fine desks. Plainness of exterior was compensated for by an elaborate interior, including several secret compartments ingeniously concealed. A few years ago I had an opportunity to examine a New England Queen Anne desk (see Plate LXII) of about 1740, in the collection of Richard Loeb. I found that it had no less than sixteen secret compartments, including two very small ones on the undersides of the arms that supported the slanting lid when opened. In providing such desks with these hiding places, American craftsmen outdid those of England. Possibly this reflected the proverbial lawlessness of America.

In the highboy, which appeared about 1700, American cabinetmakers found a piece that evidently pleased their clients, for they made many of them during the William and Mary, Queen Anne and Chippendale periods. In England, on the contrary, this display piece found short favor, and went out of fashion about the time George I came to the throne.

The first American highboys were of William and Mary design (see Plate LXIII). A few had spiral-turned legs, as did many of English provenance; more had the six trumpet legs which were so characteristic of the period. All were made with ball feet and braced by flat cyma-curved stretchers. Walnut was the usual wood, and drawer fronts were veneered with either crotch or burl walnut. Here our craftsmen followed the English custom of edging the drawer fronts with herringbone banding of a lighter shade of walnut, but again any attempt at marquetry was omitted. The grace with which the lower edge of the skirt was cut in triple arches was another point by which the colonial craftsmen showed that they appreciated beauty and possessed skill to incorporate such a detail in a piece.

Lowboys made in the same style and likewise of walnut usually had only four trumpet legs, although six were not unknown. In the former, the delicately turned legs were braced with crossing transverse cyma-curved stretchers. Sometimes an urn-shaped turning was mounted at the crossing for additional decoration.

Although William and Mary highboys and lowboys adhered closely to the basic design, with the Queen Anne style (see Plate LXV) came noticeable elaboration that enhanced the beauty of these companion pieces. The cabriole legs were made less stocky and were delicately curved. The pad feet varied, and the flat cornice was often replaced by a broken pediment bonnet top, complete with delicately turned flame finials. The top and bottom sections were built with central drawers, ornamented with fan or shell carving. A few of these pieces in walnut emphasized such shells further by gilding, and marked the first time that such treatment was used in America, although much of the finest walnut furniture of England was ornamented by combining gilding with carving.

American Queen Anne highboys and lowboys were also made in maple, cherry and birch (see Plate LXIX). Those of curly maple were especially popular in

PLATE LXIX

Ginsburg & Levy, Inc.
Ginsburg & Levy, Inc.
Metropolitan Museum of Art

Queen Anne Lowboys

(Top, center) Has single large drawer and well curved cabriole legs. Walnut, Pennsylvania, 1710-1720. (Above) Queen Anne mirror, walnut, carved and gilded, Pennsylvania, circa 1750. (Bottom, left) Banded walnut veneered top and drawer fronts. New England, 1715-1725. (Bottom, right) Japanned in Chinese manner on maple. Boston, circa 1735.

New England, being made almost as long as these complementary pieces remained in fashion.

No one so far has had the patience to do enough research into furniture history to establish whence came the block-front design, so successfully applied to desks, secretaries, chests of drawers and chests-on-chests in America from about 1760 to the outbreak of the Revolutionary War. Although such pieces were produced in limited number in Massachusetts and Connecticut, it was at Newport, Rhode Island, that the finest examples were made. They were the work of two closely related families, the Townsends and the Goddards, both unassuming members of the Society of Friends.

Of these, John Townsend and John Goddard were the craftsmen who made such fine pieces of block-front furniture that just the mention of them today stirs the imagination of anyone at all interested in antiques. The block-front design, as they interpreted it, consisted of three parallel panels extending up the front of the piece. The central panel was slightly depressed, with the other two in balancing relief. At the top of each was a finely done shell carving, always of eleven rays, either incised or raised to match the panel beneath. In desks or secretaries the interior was adorned with narrower panels and carved shells repeating the treatment of the front.

Although block-front pieces were made well after the start of the Chippendale period, their detail was essentially in the Queen Anne tradition. The square bracket feet, the moldings, the restrained ornamentation, all served to place them as Queen Anne survival pieces, made approximately twenty years after Chippendale's designs had become fashionable here. Walnut was the favored wood, though mahogany was accepted toward the end.

Another Queen Anne survival was the kneehole, made as a desk, a man's dressing table or a combination of both (see Plate LXX). Townsend and Goddard ornamented them with characteristic sets of three carved shells and called them "buro" tables. Similarly, they made a number of small three-drawer chests of drawers, probably as companion pieces to their block-front chest-on-chests (see Plate LVI) or to the "buro" tables just mentioned.

Kneehole pieces were also made by contemporaries of Townsend and Goddard, from Massachusetts to Maryland, but the designs were simpler. The carved shells were omitted; and blocking, if included, was not so well executed. All of them, however, had a cupboard with a simple paneled door at the rear of the kneehole itself, which served most conveniently as a place where a gentleman might store his wig, carefully combed and brushed on its block.

From the beginning of the William and Mary period, the appeal of furniture decorated in the Chinese manner or of lacquered pieces brought back from China was very strong in England and rapidly manifested itself in America, where men who specialized in the art were following their trade as early as 1700, especially

PLATE LXX

Ginsburg & Levy, Inc.
Ginsburg & Levy, Inc.
Hyman Kaufman
Gallery of Fine Arts, Yale University

Kneehole Desks

(Top, left) Made in New York City of mahogany, circa 1770. (Top, right) Block-front, made by Ebenezer Calef, cabinetmaker of Nantucket, Massachusetts, 1760-1770.

Small Block-front Furniture

(Bottom, left) Chest of drawers by John Townsend, Rhode Island, 1760-1770. (Bottom) Slant-top desk attributed to Benjamin Burnham of Connecticut. Cherry, 1765-1775.

in Boston. Such a one was David Mason, who advertised in the *Boston News Letter:* "Jappanner, does all sorts of Jappanning, varnishing, Painting and gilding." To Mason and men like him, cabinetmakers would send the highboys, lowboys, secretaries, chests of drawers and mirror frames that they had made of maple or pine to be ornamented with a colorful decoration depicting Chinese garden scenes, landscapes, people, birds and animals (see Plates LXIV, LXV, LXIX, LXXI).

So closely did these japanners approximate the Chinese spirit that it is hard to believe they know nothing of the Orient at first hand, but had only some manual published in London early in the eighteenth century to guide them. Japanned furniture was made in such large towns as Boston, New York and Philadelphia from the beginning to the middle of the eighteenth century, though the best work seems to have been done before 1735. After that date the tendency was to do routine work without careful attention to decorative details. However, much of this japanning was of as high quality as London work.

Of the handsome Oriental lacquered cabinets, supported by elaborately carved and gilded stands, which were so popular in England, not one appears to have found its way across the Atlantic. The reason is simple. There was no direct commerce between America and the Chinese treaty ports until the latter years of the eighteenth century. The cabinets were expensive at best, and importing one from London would have been almost prohibitive for even the wealthiest of the colonists. So they apparently contented themselves with the japanned pieces and other display furniture made by native craftsmen.

For some time it was thought that all William and Mary, Queen Anne and most Chippendale looking-glasses found in this country were imported from England or Europe. Contemporary newspaper advertisements listed mirrors and other decorative household accessories as "lately come from London in the ship——" to be sold at this or that dealer's shop. But though looking-glass makers had to depend on Vauxhall in England or on Continental sources for the silvered mirror glass, from about 1700 on, some few craftsmen made American versions of the William and Mary looking-glasses. These usually had simple molded walnut frames surmounted by an arch-shaped ornamental top, cut in Flemish scrolls or cyma curves, and sometimes pierced as well (see Plate LXI). They were small—about two by three feet—because of the great cost of mirror glass. Such mirrors are very rare today and to find one with glass in original condition is a great accomplishment.

By about 1720, American looking-glass makers had increased in number and were working in the Queen Anne style. In this the silvered glass was generally in two parts. The top one was arch-shaped and usually decorated with wheel-cut engraving in a conventionalized pattern. The lower glass was oblong. Both had polished beveled edges. At first the frames were simple convex moldings, some of walnut and others of native soft wood painted to imitate walnut. Shortly after,

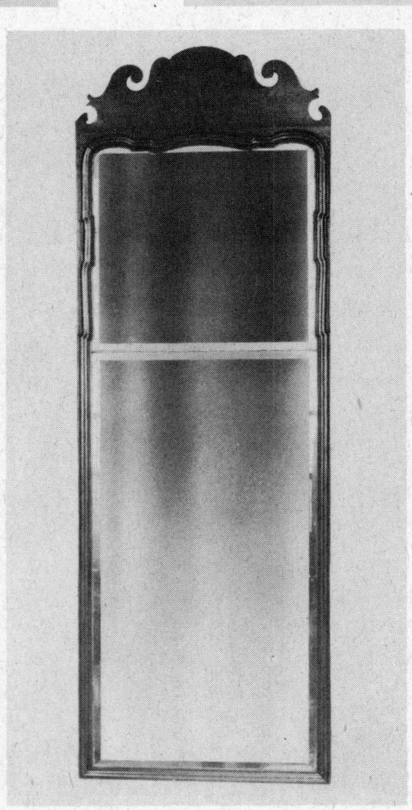

PLATE LXXI

Ginsburg & Levy, Inc.
Ginsburg & Levy, Inc.
Metropolitan Museum of Art
Philadelphia Museum

Early American Mirrors

(Top, left) William and Mary, frame of walnut oyster veneer. New England, 1700-1720. (Bottom, left) Queen Anne, arched frame of pine painted to imitate grained walnut veneer. Possibly Philadelphia, circa 1730. (Right, top) Queen Anne, japanned frame with carved and gilded shell. Boston, circa 1735. (Right bottom) Labeled John Elliot mirror, walnut. Philadelphia, 1760-1775.

and notably in Boston, large-size looking-glasses began to appear, with the frame either of partially carved and gilded walnut, or of pine japanned in imitation of Chinese work. These mirrors were oblong and had a shaped top. If shell-carved, the shells were gilded, and there was usually a line of gilding on the inner edge of the frame (see Plate LXXI).

Queen Anne looking-glasses continued to be made well into the Chippendale years, as is evidenced by the labeled ones made by John Elliott, who worked in Philadelphia from 1753 to 1776 and used a bilingual label—English and German—to attract the Pennsylvania Dutch trade. He not only made looking-glasses in his shop on Walnut Street, but imported more ornate ones from London. Therefore a looking-glass bearing his label might be either imported or made here. If rather simple as to decoration, it would be of American provenance; if ornate, an eighteenth-century importation. In either case, the looking-glass in question would rank as an American antique either by virtue of birth or adoption.

CHAPTER XIII

FAKING AND LEGITIMATE RESTORING

IN PART I, Mr. Symonds warns his readers against the counterfeit walnut pieces. What he has said can well be re-read if one intends to collect English walnut furniture, either in Great Britain or in the United States. For certain English cabinetmakers, working from about 1900 or earlier until the beginning of World War II, were real artists in their ability to counterfeit the antique. But they always left traces of their working ways that, once understood, could be readily recognized.

As to American furniture of the same style, it would be idle to say that counterfeits have not been made in the past or that others will not be produced in the future. But so far, such faking has been done by isolated repairmen or unscrupulous dealers working independently. They did their own counterfeiting and selling. Nor did they make an entire assortment—just a piece here and another there, and none repeated frequently because it sold well.

Faking of American antique furniture made between 1690 and 1750 has so far been done as individual pieces, made occasionally when suitable wood was available or the wreck of a good piece came to hand to serve as the starting point for an extensive reconstruction. During the past twenty years I have been in a number of city and country antique shops, often in the workrooms, as far south as Virginia and as far west as Ohio. Nowhere do I know of a clique of repairmen and dealers who make a practice of faking American furniture.

There are at least three reasons for this. First, thoroughly careful faking costs too much at present wage scales to be profitable. Second, American collectors are too well informed; they know too much about earmarks of the genuine and counterfeit furniture. Lastly, there are still enough genuine pieces available in the rough at prices competitive with those the faker would have to charge.

The nearest we have to a fake antique clique in the United States are several men who operate large repair shops. They use power-driven machinery and their workmen are not skilled craftsmen. Into these "factories" are fed quantities of ordinary country furniture, made about 1800 to 1830. These pieces are taken apart and rebuilt to look like William and Mary or Queen Anne antiques. But the workmanship is low grade and the "antique" produced deceives no one who knows anything at all about genuine antiques.

PLATE LXXII

Ginsburg & Levy, Inc.
Formerly Herbert Lawton Collection
Metropolitan Museum of Art

Rare Queen Anne Clock

By William Fitz, Portsmouth, New Hampshire, circa 1769, its cherry case with reeded column pilasters, arched dial opening and doorway, follows English architectural design of forty years earlier.

Unique William and Mary Cabinet

Made for Colonel John Wainwright of Ipswich, Massachusetts, who died in 1708, this small walnut cabinet has no known duplicate of New England provenance.

Pennsylvania Dutch Dresser of Walnut

Rhine Valley tradition with American adaptations. Cornice, double paneled doors, center tier of five drawers and three block feet, showing individuality of Pennsylvania Dutch cabinetmakers.

As outlets, these fakers use certain roving auctioneers who know very well what they are selling. In a miscellaneous two or three days' sale a good proportion of these "rebuilts" are "planted," possibly one out of every ten or fifteen lots. When the auctioneer is crying one of these counterfeits, he works fast and uses a patter that only seems to guarantee the piece as genuine. Sales of this sort are referred to as "seeded," and the most desired buyers are those who know nothing about antiques. Indeed, they are the only ones apt to be deceived by furniture so completely and poorly rebuilt that nothing of the genuine antique remains.

In buying American antique furniture of the period under discussion, there a few things the collector should observe before making a purchase. The ball or turned feet of many pieces, such as tables, chairs, highboys and the like, may not all be original. Time and normal wear have taken their toll. So one or more of the feet may be replaced. This is a legitimate restoration, provided the piece is not sold as completely original. The same holds with pieces having carved Spanish feet.

In the case of tables, look at the top. It may be a replacement, and this would cut the price of the piece materially. Then there are the pieces with brass drawer handles and keyhole plates. Most of them through the years will have lost some or all of their original brasses. Replacing them with reproductions is legitimate, provided they are not represented as the originals. Obviously a William and Mary highboy with all its original tear-drop brasses is a rarity, and will be priced accordingly.

The same holds true of any piece with original varnish or other finish still in usable condition. Under no circumstances should such a piece be refinished. Where refinishing is necessary, the motto should be "how little" rather than "how much," since too vigorous scraping and sandpapering can destroy the patina that age, and age alone, can give.

In butterfly and tavern tables and similar pieces, the original drawer pulls were wooden knobs. These should be preserved or, if missing, replaced with new ones that are copies made for that purpose. In Queen Anne highboys, lowboys and chairs with cabriole legs and pad feet, make sure the legs are original and that the feet are not new work, skillfully glued and spliced. Of course, one leg or foot replacement would be considered a proper restoration, but not all four. In such a case, the piece passes over into the rebuilt or over-restored class. Also in the highboys or chests-on-chests, a proper example is one in which the top and bottom sections started out together. Those assembled of odd tops and bases recut to fit are also rebuilts, and have little value as antiques.